Visions of Community in the Pre-Modern World

VISIONS

OF

COMMUNITY

IN THE

PRE-MODERN WORLD

Edited by
NICHOLAS HOWE

UNIVERSITY OF NOTRE DAME PRESS
Notre Dame, Indiana

Copyright © 2002
University of Notre Dame
Notre Dame, Indiana 46556
All Rights Reserved
http://www.undpress.nd.edu

Manufactured in the United States of America

Library of Congress Cataloging-in-Publication Data
Visions of community in the pre-modern world / edited
by Nicholas Howe
p.   cm.
Includes bibliographical references and index.
ISBN 0-268-02862-1 (cloth : alk. paper)
ISBN 0-268-02863-x (pbk. : alk. paper)
1. Community—History—Case studies.
2. Religious communities—History—Case studies.   I. Howe,
Nicholas (Nicholas George), 1953– .
HM756 .V57   2002
307'.09—dc21

2002003992

∞ *This book is printed on acid-free paper.*

Contents

Acknowledgments

In the course of preparing this volume for publication, I have had the invaluable assistance of Suzanne Childs and Wendy Matlock of the Center for Medieval and Renaissance Studies at the Ohio State University. I am deeply grateful to them for their meticulous work and good cheer. Barbara Hanrahan and Carole Roos of the University of Notre Dame Press have seen this volume through its various stages with great efficiency. Finally, I thank the contributors to this volume for their patience and support.

Nicholas Howe

Introduction

Nicholas Howe

A real community is unshakeable, indubitable, and enduring. . . . It remains unaffected and whole even when the people united by it are already in their graves.

—*Nadezhda Mandelstam*

Both as ideal and social form, community defines a necessary space between the isolated individual and the anonymous mass. Despite the clichés that threaten to overwhelm it, community still matters as a term because it identifies a group of people having a common purpose or identity as well as some shared knowledge of each other. The larger the community, the more tenuous these common or shared elements are likely to become, or the more abstract. When stretched to include the contemporary nation-state, the use of community as a term of praise reads metaphorically rather than literally, as is evident from Benedict Anderson's frequently quoted definition of imagined community: "It is *imagined* because the members of even the smallest nation will never know most of their fellow-members, meet them, or even hear of them, yet in the minds of each lives the image of their communion."[1] The larger the group becomes, the more likely it is that the source of its "communion" will become imagined or tenuous or abstract. This process of growth may also make for greater longevity, especially because those communities which fail to develop a critical mass of members sooner or later fade into nothingness. At a certain moment in its existence, a community must expand beyond its initial, formative stage in order to survive. This growth in membership may well bring with it some loss or dilution of identity, but that may also contribute to its survival over the turn of generations. For the same energy or fervor that once inspired the creation of a community can grow divisive over time or, simply, too burdensome for those who come later.

Communities are in a foundational sense manifestations of the local, even after they spread across cultures, peoples, and languages to become, for instance, a great world religion. A global community like Islam or Christianity must remain deeply attached to the memory of its originary place and community precisely because it has grown to encompass so much territory and so many followers. The more universal the claims of the community, the more likely it is to idealize or commemorate its founders as a group. For the communities of pre-modern Europe, such as those studied in this book, the most apposite example of an originary community would be the apostles surrounding Christ at the Last Supper. For that reason, the congregation endures as a significant unit of community within Christendom (however it is defined doctrinally) because it asserts the importance of the local, as viewed by both historical and contemporary measures. The parish of a Catholic church exists as a community in the here and now (say, in Columbus, Ohio) but also as a historical allusion or recognition of an earlier community, as is signaled by its name (as in Holy Family or St. Francis of Assisi). Among Protestant denominations, especially those that resist centralized organization, the congregation is all the more self-evidently a local community. This element is particularly evident among those American church-communities that name themselves by some feature of their immediate location (as in Crestview Presbyterian Church) or by their order of establishment (First A.M.E. Zion Church of Columbus).

The subject of community presents itself in various ways that are often easier to distinguish in the abstract than in actual practice. There are instances of community in the form of social groups, such as local parishes or political parties or fans of a team; and there are desired evocations of community in the form of social ideals, such as appeals to national unity or political change or religious reform. At the level of daily life, most instances of community embody both the actual and the desired, though the balance between the two may vary from member to member in a given example. Evocations of community in our culture often have a vaguely nostalgic cast to them, reminding us that "nostalgia" once referred to the melancholia or sickness of being apart from one's literal home (*nostos*), from one's originary and sustaining community. In the late-modernist and post-modernist styles of recent years, "community" has been used as a politically neutral (that is, non-reactionary) term to evoke that idyllic form of social being which, at its most desirable, once made for a golden age. Historians and theorists too sophisticated or skeptical to indulge in traditionalist dreams of a lost world may thus still venture to evoke community as a worthy social and political ideal.

In the face of ideological hegemony or cultural conformity, the dream of community can be summoned to support liberating values of egalitarianism, harmony, connectedness. Such images of community have become a way of protecting ourselves against the anonymity of post-modern society and the isolation of extreme individuality. There is also something engagingly voluntary about this contemporary sense of community; it conveys the idea that we can belong, each of us, to different communities at the same moment in our lives (for example, families, professions, religions, political parties, genders, sexualities, neighborhoods) as well as to different communities across the span of our lives (for example, schools, churches, neighborhoods, social circles). Precisely because we are not fixed in a single community, we find it a compelling word for celebrating how we wish to live now. To speak of "a sense of community" is to articulate an image of belonging, of rootedness, perhaps even of happiness.

What sometimes seems obscured or lost by our use of this term is the historical dimension that adheres to community as an ideal. I do not mean that we lose sight of the history of a given community; to the contrary, that sense of history or tradition is often what draws people to enter a given community. Thus, some Catholics will seek out a parish where they can attend a Latin Mass, or residents of a neighborhood will band together to preserve its historical character against developers. By "historical dimension" I mean something different: our own image of community comes to be so inevitable or natural in our thinking that it seems to exist as a constant across cultures and eras. It was in large measure to interrogate this ahistorical sense of community that the scholars in this volume were invited to speak in a lecture series on "Communities and Identities in the Pre-Modern World" sponsored in

1997–98 by the Center for Medieval and Renaissance Studies at the Ohio State University. They were asked to address this large topic in the ways that each found most engaging. The lectures that they gave as well as the chapters that grew out of them may be read as a set of case-studies for exploring ideas and manifestations of community between the eleventh and sixteenth centuries. These studies range geographically from Europe to regions of Islam in Africa and the Near East, and also to regions of Latin America conquered by the Spanish. While acknowledging the large factors that affect community—such as religious belief, imperial expansion, warfare—these studies focus on precise examples and moments in the pre-modern world. In that regard, they offer implicit responses to current historians or theorists of nationalism who homogenize or reify the medieval and renaissance periods as ages of religious identity or pre-nationalism in order to valorize their own claims for the exceptional nature of modern experience. Yet it would be limiting to read the chapters in this book merely as refuting claims for modern exceptionalism. For each chapter studies on its own terms the ways in which people in earlier centuries defined, preserved, and represented their forms of social, political, and religious communities.

Although the title for this lecture series referred to "communities and identities," it was the first of these terms that proved most compelling to the contributors. Each of them, with no editorial prompting, chose that term to appear in her or his title: "Individualism and Institutions in Medieval Religious Communities" (Giles Constable), "Visual Communities in Byzantium and Medieval Islam" (Anthony Cutler), "'Illustris patriarcha Joseph': Jean Gerson, Representations of Saint Joseph, and Imagining Community among Churchmen in the Fifteenth Century" (Pamela Sheingorn), "Catholic Communities and Their Art" (Annabel Patterson), and "Cartography and Community in the Hispanic World" (Richard Kagan). Readers of this volume will notice, however, that the question of identities did not disappear from the studies themselves. Indeed each of the contributors argues in varying ways that communities are means to establish and enact and maintain identities. Put another way, community is often the immediately recognizable form or manifestation taken by identity because it is displayed in the actual world. The frequent references to visual materials in the following essays suggest that it is highly appropriate to speak of the matter of display, for much of the work of community-formation was accomplished in the medieval and renaissance periods through visual materials and strategies.

The communities surveyed in this volume were, of course, constructed to include as well as to exclude. If one thinks of monastic communities configured by gender, one can see that the same community could accomplish both inclusion and exclusion at the same moment. Yet, there were far more subtle and haunting acts of exclusion in the shaping and maintaining of monastic communities. Thus, as Giles Constable notes in his essay, when communities of monks became more and more fixed as institutions, they lost some of their original austerity and provoked dissent from some long-time members who resented the formalization of community and the establishment of an explicit rule. The solutions to this problem were numerous, as Constable notes, but the dilemma itself may be read as paradigmatic of the way communities often evolve. As revolutionary sects become institutionalized in the form of political parties, they face this same dilemma. Their examples of singularity, to use the medieval term for those who stand apart from this process of institutionalization, are likely to be imprisoned, sent into exile, or executed. Releasing monks of a singular character so that they might become hermits or join another group of recluses seems a much kinder solution.

Communities, as the example of monastic groups suggests, are not eternally fixed entities. Rather, they have what may be described as predictable life-cycles by which they are formed and then re-formed in response to changing circumstances in the larger world around them as well as to changing notions among each group as to what defines it as a community. Constable points out, for instance, that monastic communities came to define their membership not so much on the basis of stability of location, that a monk was bound by his vow to a particular place, as on the basis of stability of profession, that a monk was bound by a vow of service to God. And this was a vow that could by its very nature be honored anywhere within God's creation.

This act of redefining community by its purpose rather more than by its location reminds us that communities are, finally, groups of like-minded individuals who have agreed to define their fundamental beliefs or interpret their central texts in similar ways. Those who cannot agree with such definitions or interpretations endanger the harmony of the community; they are cast out as heretics, dissidents, counter-revolutionaries, sociopaths, weirdoes. In his study of Byzantine and Islamic communities, Anthony Cutler develops a crucial point in this regard when he observes that we as modern scholars must struggle with what each group understood its textual and visual signs to mean at the time they circulated— even when those meanings are far removed from their original or etymological signification. Such root meanings are of compelling interest to us as scholars, at least in part because they allow us to exercise critical ingenuity, but they may also be irrelevant to the ways in which signs served to bind interpreters into a community.

The force of visual signs such as icons to assert the orthodox beliefs of a dominant culture is perhaps most evident from Byzantine examples that stood at the center of the church, whether we consider it as a group of believers or as a physical structure (consider the ikonostasis). Visual images and representations were no less powerful when pressed into service by an endangered minority community, such as that of English Catholics during the Reformation. Annabel Patterson argues a striking parallel between the portrait painters who represented members of that same Catholic community and the missionary priests who belonged to it: both assumed responsibility for defining and consolidating the community of Catholics. In this threatened culture, visual representations served as incitements to conversion and likewise aided in maintaining the community. More radically, if perhaps more implicitly, these representations were meant ultimately to reinstate the community of the English as a people within the larger community of the Roman Catholic Church. That this imperiled community of English Catholics was aristocratic and wealthy gives another dimension to Patterson's case-study, for it establishes that what seems at first glance to be a luxury good—portraits painted in oil by eminent artists rather than competent craftsmen— could serve urgent political and religious ends.

To achieve these highly partisan purposes of evoking community, portraits of English Catholics by Van Dyck and other painters establish their own sets of signs. These are the images that modern scholars must learn to recognize if they are to identify the non- or meta-aesthetic work done by such paintings. In his survey of city images and maps in the Hispanic world of Europe and the Americas,

Richard Kagan offers the useful term "communicentric" for those images that were designed from within to establish and represent communities to the outside world. Such images were called into being, to use his example, for communities that were either newly founded or newly registered by the Spanish colonial imagination. That communicentric images are parochial in their proud representation of community may well explain the need for them in times and places of cultural contact. Under such circumstances, communities defended previously along strict lines of race, religion, language become more permeable and mixed. Moreover, as Kagan's study suggests, a community can attain a greater authority and presence in the cultural imagination when it becomes registered on a map or artistic view of the city, for these are the genres best able to authenticate the place of a community in the world.

It is for self-evident reasons easier to study communities that survive over time than those that do not: they make a greater mark on the cultural memory and thus loom larger in the imagination of later historians. They are also, and this is no small matter, likely to leave behind more evidence to be studied, sometimes even in the form of living members. It is thus all the more valuable to have in this volume a study of a less than successful attempt to reinvent a religious community, that envisioned by the fifteenth-century French theologian Jean Gerson. He sought, as Pamela Sheingorn demonstrates, to restore Christian morality through the agency of male authority. More precisely, he sought to refigure the Holy Family by giving a far greater role to Joseph than he had previously enjoyed. Behind this refiguration lay Gerson's profound anxiety at the increasing influence claimed by women as a community of interpreters and teachers within the Catholic Church. Faced with the rise of a new and threatening interpretive community, Gerson proposed to convert Joseph from comic cuckold to honored father of a family, that foundational model for so many other forms of community. If Gerson's attempt to reshape the idea of Christian community through the resources of the patriarchal family did not succeed, his attempt identifies one further characteristic of communities: they are not easy to manage or reshape when pressure for change manifests itself through an emerging new community that seems to hold out a better hope for achieving the possibilities of life.

The inherent complexity and variety of communities within even a reasonably defined period such as pre-modern Europe may be read as a powerful argument against sweeping generalizations about the ways in which human beings form themselves into more or less coherent groups. This conclusion is immediately evident from the five case-studies in this volume. Indeed, more such studies would serve chiefly to illustrate this conclusion with different examples of community constructed along other class, political, religious, social, and geographical categories. The purpose of this volume is thus finally to encourage further explorations of the communities in which the men and women of the medieval and renaissance periods shaped ways to live on this earth.

NOTE

1. Benedict Anderson, *Imagined Communities: Reflections on the Origin and Spread of Nationalism*, rev. ed. (London and New York, 1991), 6.

CHAPTER ONE

Individualism and Institutions in Medieval Religious Communities

Giles Constable

The tension in religious communities is usually kept under control by obedience to a rule and acceptance of hierarchical authority, but it occasionally breaks out in manifestations of resistance and individualism, or singularity, as it was known in the Middle Ages. In this essay I want to study how this tension manifested itself, first, in the lives of individuals who were torn between their desire to serve God in their own way and the requirements of organized religious life and, second, within communities as the founders grew old and the members felt the need to adopt some rules and institutional structures. Similar difficulties are found in secular associations of people who come together for a common professional, political, cultural, economic, or charitable purpose. Each recruit comes to some extent with his or her own agenda, which has to be accommodated to those of others, whether they form a new group or join an established organization. Many associations founder owing to failure of leadership, to disagreements, or to the waning enthusiasm and dedication of members faced with the problems of compromise and institutionalization. First there is a secretary to communicate with members and to organize activities, then a president, elections, committees, annual dues, meetings and conferences, a newsletter or journal, and finally a building. Those who join the group along the way often have little in common with the founders, who thus find themselves in an unexpected and often unwanted position either of accepting the changes or of striking out again on their own. So it was with many people who were drawn to the religious life in the Middle Ages, and it is with their aspirations, frustrations, and accommodations that I am concerned here.

I

Entry to religious life was in principle free and voluntary. According to both the rule of Benedict and the so-called rule of the Master, which is now generally recognized as the principal source of the rule of Benedict, the promise or profession, as it came to be called, of those who entered a religious community was a personal commitment to God and the saints, the patrons of the community, and not a vow in the later sense of the term.[1] In the rule of the Master the abbot said to a new monk that "You promise nothing to me, but to God and to this oratory or sacred altar," and in the rule of Benedict the promise was made "in the presence of God and His saints."[2] Cassian in his *Conferences*, which was another important source for the rule of Benedict, emphasized the liberty of those leading a religious life and the broader freedom (*libertas largior*) of those who chose to live as hermits. True liberty is found only where the Lord is, he wrote later, citing Paul's dictum that "Where the spirit of the Lord is, there is liberty."[3] Even the system of oblation by which children were given by their parents to God and a monastery was not seen as infringing the freedom of entry to religious life but as opening the way to a higher liberty, since the oblates were free gifts to God made when they were too young to make the commitment themselves, like baptism, which was often compared to entering religious life.[4]

This view was generally accepted in the Middle Ages, even by those who knew that in fact many people entered and remained in monasteries against their wills.[5] A charter from the abbey of the Trinity at Vendôme in about 1070 declared that it was "praiseworthy and useful to submit to his [God's] service by free will (*spontanea voluntate*) rather than compulsory need" and that "Many men considering this, although they were free according to the servile freedom of the world, gave themselves freely (*sponte*) to the free servitude of their Creator."[6] According to St. Anselm of

Canterbury, liberty was the power to preserve the rectitude of the will, and there was a hierarchy of liberties stretching from a worldly liberty without rectitude to the supreme liberty of God.[7] At the bottom of the hierarchy were people who, though legally free, were in fact ruled by their passions. Somewhere in the middle were monks, who were in principle free to serve God. The liberty of monks, said Abelard in his sermon on John the Baptist, which was written about 1127/8, resembled that given to the onager or wild ass by the Lord, who in Job 39:5 "sent out the wild ass free" and "loosed his bonds." Just as the wild ass is freer than the domestic ass because it bears no burdens and is not bound by chains, so monks are more free the further they are from servitude to secular affairs.[8] No one could be forced to enter the religious life, according to Peter of Blois, because the freedom of spiritual marriage is greater than the freedom of carnal marriage, which by the time Peter was writing was guaranteed in both ecclesiastical and secular law.[9]

In the early Middle Ages, and even as late as the twelfth century, it was not uncommon to enter religious life without making a formal profession, simply by wearing the monastic habit—*solo habitu*, as it was called. After Guibert of Nogent's father died in the mid-1060s, his mother retired first to a manor belonging to the bishop of Beauvais and then to the abbey of St. Germer de Flay, where she lived in a little house and subjected herself to an old woman who wore the habit of a nun and gave a great appearance of religion. Among other things, she learned the seven penitential psalms "by hearing not by seeing," Guibert said, presumably because she was illiterate, and she turned them over in her mind day and night, "chewing them with such savor" that the sweet song of her sighs and groans unceasingly filled the ears of God.[10] Women like this who lived as nuns without making a profession or promise of obedience posed a problem for ecclesiastical authorities. When king Harold of England's daughter Gunnilda abandoned her monastic habit, Anselm wrote her that

> Although you were not consecrated by a bishop and did not read a profession in his presence, the fact that you wore publicly and privately the habit of the holy undertaking (*propositum*) . . . is itself a manifest and undeniable profession. For before the profession and consecration of the monastic way of life that are now usual were made, many thousands of people of both sexes

professed by their habit alone that they were of this way of life and attained its height and crown. And whoever casts off this habit taken without this profession and consecration were judged apostates.[11]

At about the same time, the canon lawyer and bishop Ivo of Chartres wrote that a monk was made "by contempt for the world and complete love of God" and that profession and benediction were not sacraments but rather guarantees against backsliding, "since all stability in religion, unless it is strictly bound and conserved, flourishes when it is new and rare and grows old and worthless with age and popularity."[12]

Anselm and Ivo were two of the most influential churchmen of their day, and in these passages they expressed the view that even if monks and nuns in principle entered religious life voluntarily, or even informally, and enjoyed a higher state of freedom than existed in the secular world, they were in practice irrevocably bound to their commitment. According to the rule of Benedict, which governed the lives of most (though by no means all) monks and nuns after the ninth century, a new monk promised "stability and *conversatio morum* and obedience."[13] There is, and was even in the Middle Ages, some doubt about the meaning of *conversatio morum*, which may mean either a turning away or conversion in the modern sense or (as I tend to believe) a turning to a religious way of life, including both chastity and poverty, which at that time were not mentioned in the promise. There was no doubt, however, about the meaning of obedience or of stability, which was commonly taken until at least the twelfth century to mean remaining until death in the house where the promise was made.[14] The only implied exceptions in the rule are, first, the requirement that a monk from a known monastery should not be received without the consent of his abbot and a letter of recommendation, which suggests that transfers with such consent were allowed, and, second, a reference in the final chapter to the rule as the beginning of *conversatio* and the statement that "For him who would hasten to the perfection of *conversatio*, there are the doctrines of the holy fathers, of which the observance leads a man to the height of perfection." What the height of perfection meant is again uncertain, but it opened a way for a monk to leave his monastery for a different type of religious life, either in another community or in solitude as a hermit.[15]

Hermits were traditionally regarded as even freer than monks and nuns. St. William of Malavale, the founder of the Williamites, was said to have made no profession or promise of obedience and to have lived "without dependence on the will of another," like the early hermits who were not called monks "owing to the lack of subjection and obedience."[16] Pope Hadrian IV permitted St. Gerlac to be a hermit on his own lands without becoming a monk and therefore without owing obedience to any superior.[17] Hermits were indeed often criticized for their lack of obedience. St. Romuald in his *Life* by Peter Damiani told a hermit who claimed to be free from any foreign rule (*imperium*) that he should seek the consent of his abbot and live under his governance (*dominium*), and Ivo of Chartres wrote that "The life of solitude is inferior because it is voluntary and filled with improper thoughts."[18] Bernard of Clairvaux was likewise not well disposed toward the solitary life of hermits unless it was preceded by a period in a community and unless the hermit remained under the control of an abbot. For him, as for many religious leaders of the twelfth century, the overriding obligations of those leading a religious life were obedience and lack of self-will.[19]

Anselm held that no one could abandon the religious life, however it was entered. He wrote to the novice Lanzo that

Whoever applies himself to the undertaking of cenobites should study with the whole intention of his mind to root himself with the roots of love in whatever monastery he will have made his profession, unless it is such that he is unwillingly forced to do evil there, and he should refuse to judge the ways of others or the customs of the place even if they seem useless, provided they are not against divine commands. Let him rejoice that he has at last found a place where he has decided to remain, a willing volunteer (*non invitum sed voluntarium*), for his whole life, without any consideration of moving, in order that he may be quiet and free only for performing the exercises of a pious life.

Anselm went on to urge Lanzo to reject any idea that he might lead a better life elsewhere and thus in effect closed the small escape-door left open in the rule of Benedict.[20] The duty of obedience was so great for Anselm that a monk must obey an order from his abbot to leave his monastery for business in the world, because the omissions in his monastic life will be "all swallowed up in the worth of the obedience that he practices."[21]

Even a promise made in ignorance by a child was binding according to a text attributed to Pope Urban II, who maintained that all members of a community, whether or not they had taken a vow of poverty, were obliged to lead a common life like that of the apostles.

> But someone may say that "I did not promise to lead the apostolic life, but to live according to the new customs of that monastery and according to the traditions of those fathers," or that "I did not understand thus, for I was a boy." But if you did not understand you nonetheless made the vow. . . . Search the Scriptures [in the words of John 7:52], search your rule, and see what you promised.

Urban then cited the parallel of an adult who is bound by the obligations of baptism.[22] According to Urban's successor Paschal II, "The status of monks is entirely separated from the world. Other men are allowed to serve God and not to leave the world, but monks are allowed to have neither the body nor the will in their own power (*in propria potestate*) so that the will of the Lord may be fulfilled in them."[23] Paschal did not go on to cite, like so many of his contemporaries, the dictum that "Where the spirit of the Lord is, there is liberty," but implicit in his words is the view that a monk who fulfills the will of God, rather than himself, is freer than a man in the world.

This life may appear to have allowed very little room for individualism and self-expression, but it would be a mistake to assume that religious life in the Middle Ages was always strictly and uniformly regulated, without any opportunity for individualism. Many monasteries had dependent hermitages and priories where the life was more relaxed than in the mother houses. The number of priories multiplied in the eleventh and twelfth centuries, and they served not only as units of agricultural exploitation but also as places to which members of a community, including occasional misfits, could go or be sent for longer or shorter vacations or retreats.[24] The term 'vacation' as it is used today, indeed, derives from *vacare*, which meant to be free or at peace, and was a favorite word in monastic spirituality.

There was also room for individualism and private ascetic practices within many communities. St. Oswald when he was a young man at Fleury was given, according to his *Life* by Eadmer,

> a secret place in the church where in the manner of his way of life (*pro modo conversationis suae*) he was joined more intimately to God and where he was accustomed to devote himself, removed from the disturbance of other men, to prayer, meditation, and contemplation of the eternal life.[25]

Ordericus Vitalis recorded a tradition that when St. Evroul wanted to devote himself to contemplation more ardently (*ardentius*) than he could, presumably, in the community, he went to a special chapel that was "pleasant (*amenus*) and well-suited for a solitary life."[26]

The abbey of Cluny is often considered as a model of monastic regularity, where the monks all did everything in exactly the same way, and at great length. This view is based to a great extent on the elaborate customaries of the second half of the eleventh century and on a few well-known passages by famous writers. Peter Damiani spent a week at Cluny in the mid-eleventh century and praised it in his *Gallic journey* for its order, asceticism, and regular strictness. He compared it both to the early church, where there was one heart in a multitude of believers, and to the Egyptian desert, saying that he saw at Cluny many Pauls and Anthonies (referring to the early hermits) who, though they did not live in solitude, won the prize of anchorites by imitating their works.[27] He wrote to the Cluniacs that "When I remember the strictness and fullness of your holy way of life, I consider that the teaching of the Holy Spirit and not the effort of the human invention is present." During the entire day, he continued, scarcely a half-hour was free for the monks to converse in the cloister.[28] Eadmer likewise tells us that when Anselm decided to become a monk,

> He turned over in his mind where he could best bring to pass what he desired, and he argued thus with himself: "Well then, I shall become a monk. But where? If at Cluny or at Bec, all the time I have spent in learning letters will be lost. For at Cluny the strictness of the order and at Bec the outstanding ability of Lanfranc, who is a monk there, will condemn me either to fruitlessness or to insignificance."[29]

Both Damiani and Anselm used the term *districtio,* which has been taken (probably correctly) to refer to the length as well as the tightness or strictness of the order at Cluny. Damiani's comparison to the desert fathers, however, suggests that there was also room for ascetic individualism, and the fact that he asked abbot Hugh to take care of his nephew, and to send him back, he said, "with the two wives of the trivium and the quadrivium," shows that intellectual activities were not entirely neglected.[30]

There were in fact a number of idiosyncratic holy men at Cluny, who lived either inside the abbey or outside in nearby hermitages. Under the first abbot Odo, the hermit Adegrinus lived in a cave about two miles from the abbey and came to Cluny on Sundays and on the principal feast days.[31] Within the monastic enclosure there were many small chapels and crypts that may have been used for ascetic devotions and spiritual retreats.[32] Abbot Hugh was also not unsympathetic to individualism. In about 1088 he allowed the abbot and prior of St. Rigaud to leave their monastery and live on an island, where they were joined by a Cluniac monk who was skilled at fishing.[33] Hugh tried to attract ascetic holy men to Cluny, where, according to the *Life* of the hermit Anastasius, "He could both fulfill his vow and give an example of a good way of life (*conversatio*) to the other monks" and where, according to the *Life* of St. Morandus, "Almost the entire world fled at this time, as to the common refuge of piety for the spiritual renewal of its places." Anastasius for a long time led what his biographer described as "a marvelous life," remaining in the oratory when the other monks ate, getting up at night while the others slept, living on bread and water, and praying all night long on his knees. "Once a year, to celebrate Lent, he went into the solitudes or into rugged places, and then he tormented himself beyond measure with prayers, fasts, vigils, and genuflections." Both Anastasius and Morandus acted as monastic missionaries for Hugh, traveling with him and helping to spread Cluniac monasticism all over Europe.[34] At least one ascetic, Geoffrey of Chalard, turned down Hugh's invitation and became a hermit, saying that he did not want to refuse him but could not take on the burden of the monastic rule. "If I give in to the request of the holy man and enter monastic life, I shall be inconstant, for I have intended to do something else."[35] Gerald, whom Hugh appointed prior of St. Salvator at Nevers and who served as librarian (*armarius*) at Cluny and chamberlain (*procura-*

tor) at Marcigny, died in 1133. Toward the end of his life he retired, with the permission of Peter the Venerable, to a place named Aujoux (*Altum Iugum*), on account of its height. Peter wrote in his book *On Miracles* that "It transcended all the surrounding country" and afforded views of the Alps of Italy and a large part of France. There, surrounded by forests and exposed to the winds and snows, Gerald "removed himself far from human habitation and persuaded others who were seeking more remote places to seek only themselves (*nihil ultra se*) in his solitude." He occupied himself with holy works and prayer, and "free for reading he raised himself more vehemently to divine love by frequent discussion of the holy words."[36]

There was some latitude even in Cistercian houses, which tended to emphasize common life.[37] Galland of Rigny, writing in the second quarter of the twelfth century, said that a monk who on account of the heat could not work in the fields should choose—he used the term *eligere*—some work to do in the shade or in the house, and that a monk who could not celebrate all the liturgical feasts should observe at least All Saints. "Just as all the other feasts are included in the feast of All Saints," Galland wrote, "all the other [virtues] are contained in the virtue of charity."[38]

Freedom of this sort could easily be abused. Bernard in his treatise on the *Steps of humility* described in scathing terms the type of monk who strove to do more than others in order to appear superior to them and who was not satisfied with the common rule of the monastery and the example of the older monks.

> He gets more pleasure from one fast that he keeps while the others are eating than if he had fasted a week with the others. He considers one little prayer of his own more praiseworthy than the whole psalmody of a night. At dinner he keeps constantly looking around the tables, and if he sees anyone eating less [than himself], he grieves that he is beaten and begins mercilessly to deprive himself of even that food which he had planned to allow as indispensable, fearing the damage to his reputation more than the pangs of hunger. If he discovers anyone more haggard, anyone more cadaverous, he despises himself, he gets no rest. And since he cannot see his own face as others see it [There were no mirrors in medieval monasteries.] he looks at his hands and arms, which he can see, he pokes his ribs, he feels

his shoulders and loins, so that he may guess the pallor or color of his face according as he finds the limbs of his body satisfactorily emaciated or not. Zealous for himself, indifferent to the community, he keeps vigil in bed, he sleeps in the choir. While the others are saying psalms at matins, he sleeps the entire night; when the others are resting in the cloister after matins, he alone remains in the oratory; he spits and coughs; from his corner he fills the ears of those outside with groans and sighs. But although these things that he does with singularity but without sincerity raise his reputation among the more innocent, who praise the works they see without discerning whence they proceed, they are deceived when they call the miserable man blessed.[39]

Aside (one may hope) from sincerity, this behavior sounds like that of Anastasius at Cluny. Monks like this were probably not uncommon in medieval monasteries, and Bernard clearly expected his readers to recognize the type.

Two factors that promoted the expression of individualism, though not necessarily of singularity, in twelfth-century monasticism were, first, the tendency, especially in reformed houses, to exclude children and accept as recruits only adults of sixteen or sometimes twenty years of age, and, second, the replacement of the early view of stability of location by the concept of stability of profession, which required a monk to be responsible for his own salvation and to be loyal to the spirit rather than the place of his promise and profession. Anselm in the passage cited above accepted that a monk should leave a place where he was forced to do evil and should not obey customs that were opposed to divine law. The change with regard to oblation is reflected in the fact that in contrast to Urban II, who held that a vow made by a child was binding, Alexander III decreed that profession made before the age of fourteen was invalid.[40] The decision to leave the world and enter religious life thus became more personal, as did the decision to leave a particular community or type of religious life.

Moves from one monastery to another were not uncommon and were motivated by many factors. Amadeus of Hauterives was a powerful lord who in the early twelfth century entered the Cistercian abbey of Bonnevaux, together with his only son and sixteen local lords. The abbot of Bonnevaux disapproved of the liberal arts and "the lying fables of the philosophers," however, and Amadeus moved to Cluny for the sake of his son's education. Later, when the boy went to the court of his kinsman the emperor Conrad in Germany, Amadeus returned to Bonnevaux because he preferred its poverty to the rich vestments and sweet sounding chants at Cluny. He acknowledged, however, as his biographer put it, that "The congregation of this monastery shines with holy ways of life and with the greatest religion."[41] A prior of Ste-Barbe who left his monastery in order to become a regular canon wrote to his former colleagues praising the harshness and poverty of his new life, to which he had transferred, he said, "in order that my soul may always be in my own hands, that is, that my life and mind may be in my sight before myself, so that I may be mindful of God's commands."[42] A summons to leave the religious life for an administrative position often required a painful decision. When the prior of Llanthony, Robert of Bethune, was elected bishop of Hereford in 1131, according to his biographer William of Wyecombe, he compared himself to Adam expelled from paradise. "Behold how can I, seeing and willing, as it were, put myself into servitude and torments, while I am free and my own? For he who is bound by the shackles of apostolic authority does not seem to me to be free."[43]

Many of the religious leaders of the eleventh and twelfth centuries moved around and adopted distinctive, and occasionally offensive, lifestyles. The wandering preacher Robert of Arbrissel, who was a celebrated holy man and founded the abbey of Fontevrault, rejected the regular habit and wore a hair-shirt and a ragged cloak, had half-naked legs, a long beard, and his hair cut in front and was said to have lacked "only a staff of the accoutrements of a lunatic."[44] The hermit Robert of Knaresborough wore no shoes and an old white cowl over ragged clothes, and ate only greens and bread made of four parts of barley-meal and one of ashes. The monks of Headley rapidly regretted their decision to invite Robert to join them, saying that "It is hard on us to see this singular man, since he is contrary to us in our works and totally unlike us in habit and in diet." He soon returned to his hermitage, where he lived, greatly honored, until his death in 1216.[45] Stephen of Muret, the founder of the Grandmontines or "Bons hommes" of Grandmont, as they were called, described himself as "a voice crying in the wilderness" and wanted to follow his own way of poverty and self-abasement, modeled on the life of the hermits he had seen in southern Italy. He refused to be classified as a monk, canon, or hermit, which he regarded as titles of honor, and said to two visiting cardinals that "If I should glorify myself, my glory would be nothing."[46] Bernard of Tiron was also a free and restless spirit, who repeatedly escaped to a hermitage in the woods or on an island in order to avoid the obligations of ecclesiastical administration at the abbeys of St. Savin and St. Cyprien. He was clearly an admired leader, however, since the monks always sought his return. Eventually he founded the monastery of Tiron, which proved to be an influential center of reform.[47]

II

Men and women of this type were profoundly reluctant to accept ecclesiastical discipline and adopt an established rule or way of life. Many refused to do so and settled alone, or with a few like-minded companions, in remote oratories and hermitages. Countless religious communities started as hermitages or small settlements of people who sought to serve God in peace and solitude.[48] The author of the *Little book on the various orders and professions that are in the church,* which was written probably in the diocese of Liège in the second quarter of the twelfth century, said in the section on hermits, "Let no one be disturbed if a certain diversity appears in this order, and each one arranges his life differently, with some living alone, some with two or three or more, living a life that is easier for some and harder for others."[49] In order to survive, however, these communities had to institutionalize in some way or another, either as independent houses or, later, as members of religious orders, such as the Cluniacs, Cistercians, or Premonstratensians. Their members thus became formally monks or canons, or nuns or canonesses, accepted a written rule, and submitted to the authority of a superior—not always of their own selection—and sometimes also to visitors and a general chapter. Their accustomed way of life and the personal rule of their founders were thus replaced by a *vita secundum institutiones et statuta,* which imposed uniformity not only on individual communities but often throughout a congregation of religious houses.[50]

Scholars are disagreed over whether this development was the result primarily of external factors or internal pressures. There is no question that ecclesiastical authorities, and sometimes also secular powers, were suspicious of small disorganized establishments, which could not be fitted into any recognized niche in the church hierarchy and often disturbed the existing diocesan and parochial structures. There is abundant evidence of conflict over parochial and property rights between new religious houses and the local clergy and lay lords and also established monasteries, of which the interests were threatened. These suspicions culminated in the well-known decree of the Fourth Lateran Council in 1215 forbidding any new religious orders, "lest the excessive diversity of religions introduce grave confusion into the church of God," and requiring the founders of new religious houses to follow "the rule and institution of an approved religious order."[51]

Among the internal factors promoting institutionalization were the self-doubts and dissensions caused by poverty, lack (or sometimes excess) of recruits, and declining morale caused by personal disagreements, the departure of members, external hostility, and uncertainty over the future, especially as the founding members grew old. The anthropologist Mary Douglas, writing about sectarian communities in ancient Israel, said that

> At the start, while they still have their original founder, they have not had to face typical organizational problems. If such a community has survived for a generation after the death of its founder, it will have met its problems of organization and found strategies for dealing with them. The range of strategies is limited, and their adoption inaugurates the typical enclave culture which entraps its members in a self-repeating system.[52]

The same problems faced medieval religious communities, in the east as well as the west. When the founder of two monasteries on Mt. Galesios was near death, in the middle of the eleventh century, his biographer said to him

> "The brothers are afraid, father, that you will die and leave the monastery high and dry, without either having made a will or given any instructions for the two monasteries," and the father

replied, "They have no cause for fear on that score; there will be a rule, and the emperor and patriarch are going to see it."[53]

Jean Becquet said of the new orders in the Limousin that "When the founders were faced with death, their community was also faced with its future, immediate with regard to the succession, distant with regard to the form [of life]."[54]

Very little is known about the internal histories of most early medieval religious houses, but an interesting account of the development of a hermitage into a monastery is found in the charter of Louis the Pious in 819 for the abbey of Conques, which was founded at the turn of the ninth century by "a certain religious man named Dado" on the deserted site of an oratory built by some refugees from the Saracens. He cleared the land himself and was joined by another religious man named Medraldus and later by other followers who put themselves under their spiritual direction. After the congregation grew and a church was built, in the words of the charter, "It was decided by the common will (*commune voluntate*) that Dado should seek a still more remote place named Grandvabre, which he did, and that Medraldus should be made abbot and that the community should be regular," that is, adopt a rule. The emperor took the new congregation of monks under his protection and strove with God's assistance, as he put it, "that they should fight for the Lord fully under the rule of Saint Benedict both by the advice of good monks and by our frequent admonition and also by assiduously visiting this place." He gave the monastery various possessions, he said, "in order that this congregation, eternally protected by the imperial and royal defense, may be able to keep its commitment constantly . . . and pray to the Lord for us and for the common stability of our realm."[55]

Conques thus moved, within a period of less than a generation, from the fringes of Carolingian society to its center, with all the privileges and responsibilities this involved. The key steps in its evolution from a remote oratory into an imperial abbey, according to Louis's charter, were the growth of the community, the building of a church, and above all the decision "by the common will" to adopt a rule, to appoint Medraldus abbot, and to send Dado to Grandvabre. He remained associated with Conques, since Louis explicitly linked the monastery "with the said place named Grandvabre, where the aforesaid Dado had the desired peace and made an end of living." It is uncertain whether he left voluntarily or was sent away when his followers organized into a regular monastery, where he would doubtless have been out of place, since the possession of dependent churches and estates and the protection of the emperor, involving not only the responsibility to pray for him but also the advice (which may have amounted to supervision) of good monks and of the emperor himself, were incompatible with the life of a hermit.[56]

In this case the transfer was presented as uncontroversial, and the tensions created by institutionalization are often glossed over in the sources, which imply either that a rule was adopted at the beginning or that there was a smooth transition from an eremitical to a regular way of life. But behind many seemingly straightforward accounts of the foundations of monasteries and their early histories lay a tale of trouble, which can often be read only between the lines of the sources. At Prémontré, for instance, the followers of Norbert of Xanten, according to his *Life*,

> entrusted themselves to him so greatly and clung with such devotion that to obtain the glory of eternal joy they sought no order, no rule, no institutes of the holy fathers except what they heard or knew was said from his own mouth.

Norbert knew that they would need *instituta* in the future, however, and after consulting various bishops and abbots, of whom "One urged the eremitical life, one the anachoritic, one the Cistercian order," he decided on the rule of St. Augustine. No special problems were mentioned with this transfer, but it cannot have been easy, especially in view of the canons' poverty, on account of which, still according to Norbert's *Life*, "For several years they expected flight rather than a foundation of some stability."[57] At Kirkstall, an existing settlement of hermits, whose founder Seleth served as "a master and a rule," was taken over by a community of Cistercians, whose abbot Alexander urged the hermits to seek "greater perfection and a better form of life," stressing their small numbers, lack of a real master or priest, and danger of self-will. Then, after getting a grant of the land from the local lord, Alexander gathered the hermits and "drew some to himself, to be incorporated into the order; others received money and ceded to him their right and habitation." The *History of the Foundation* of Kirkstall does not say what happened to these others or to Seleth. They may have gone to another location, but they seem to have been presented with a Hobson's choice.[58]

Many new religious communities, including Cîteaux, went through some sort of crisis in their early years.[59] Dereine in his article on the "apostolic" spirituality of the founders of Afflighem defined the symptoms of crisis as the loss of the founder, opposition among the followers, instability, and a change or development of customs. "There is a complete study to be made," he said, "of the opposition between the first and second generations in foundations of the 'apostolic' type."[60] At Rolduc, disagreements developed over where the female members should live and whether to give alms to beggars or to build a church. When the founder Ailbert left and went to France, according to the *Annals* of Rolduc,

> The place was immediately humiliated and depressed by his absence and defiled by such misfortune that for many years after this it was not enlarged or elevated by building a church. Everyone who had previously loved the place by providing goods, giving council, or seeking consolation for their souls now withdrew themselves.[61]

The problems of the institutionalization of new religious communities in the early twelfth century are illustrated by three examples, or case-histories, as they might be called, from west central France: Chancelade, Fontaines-les-Blanches, and Obazine. The early history of each of these is known from a different type of source, respectively a legal document or charter, a history, and a saint's *Life*. This, and the differences between them, show that the circumstances they describe were not simply a commonplace of monastic historiography but reflected the realities of institutional development.

A summary of the history of the abbey of Chancelade was incorporated into a charter of the bishop of Périgueux in 1178,[62] where ten original members, each described as *frater* or brother, were listed by name. Six were priests (not including the future abbot Gerald of Monlava, who was probably also a priest), and three were laymen. Their first leader, who was not listed among the ten, appears to have been the former abbot of the Augustinian abbey of

Cellefrouin, named Fulcaudus (or Foucaudus). He is mentioned in 1109 and joined the group, according to the charter, "for the love of God and of holy poverty." The brothers called him abbot "on account of his sanctity and reverence" (and perhaps also his previous position), "but he was not consecrated abbot there or called the first abbot in that place . . . and there was no canonical order at Chancelade in his time, but they lived in the manner of hermits (*more heremitarum*)." In other words, they followed no recognized rule and had no formal superior. Their first chapel, which was described as "very small and made in a cheap manner," was built "next to the spring in the place of Chancelade, from which the abbey built there is now called Chancelade."

In this chapel, in 1129, probably after the death of Fulcaudus and, the charter said, "before the monastery began," bishop William made Gerald abbot at the request of all the brothers, ordained many clerics, blessed the cemetery, and donated two churches. At the same time the first stones were laid for a new church, of which William's successor, who was also named William, consecrated the first altars when they were completed. This shows the growing institutionalization and clericalization of the community and its acquisition of buildings and property. Four years later, in 1133, abbot Gerald established the canonical order at Chancelade, and "beginning to lead a regular life with the brothers committed to him," he blessed four of the founding members as the first canons: two priests, Bernard and Elias, who were respectively the first prior and second abbot, and two clerics, Elias and William, who were previously called laymen and may have been ordained in 1129. "These first men received the canonical habit and blessing from the aforesaid abbot," said the charter, "and they began to lead and held firmly until the end the first regular life in that abbey." So far this sounds like a relatively smooth transformation of a loose group of clerics and laymen leading an eremetical life under no particular rule into an organized ecclesiastical establishment.

The following sentence suggests, however, that there was disagreement in the community, since

Others who were at that time brother clerics were also present at this first blessing of the first canons, but because they did not persevere in their promise and profession up until the final day of their death but left their monastery and their brothers and did not return, they do not therefore deserve to be inscribed among those who persevered.

It is not clear whether, as the wording implies, these "other brother clerics" were blessed by Gerald as canons and subsequently left or whether they declined to participate in the ceremony. In either case, there was a split among the original members, and at least half of them (unless some had died or departed in the meantime) were not listed among the first canons. It does not require much imagination to detect a note of bitterness, not to say vindictiveness, in the charter's reference to those who "do not deserve to be inscribed among those who persevered." It cannot have been easy for a group who had once lived together as hermits, united by a common love of God and holy poverty, to have divided in this way.

A more amicable solution seems to have been reached at Fontaines-les-Blanches in Touraine, of which the history was written in about 1200 by the seventh abbot Peregrinus and which resembled Chancelade in several respects.[63] The first two hermits, who were named Geoffrey and Geoffrey *Bullonus*, settled in about 1127 in a place with many springs (hence the name *Fontanis* or Fountains), surrounded by woods, and, Peregrinus said, "very dangerous owing to the number of thieves." They were joined by a cleric named William, a knight from Flanders named Lambert the Big, and several others, including Lambert the Small, a priest named Ascelin, and a layman named David "who was pretty handy (*satis utilis*) at agriculture." Peregrinus gives some interesting details about the lives of these men, into which I cannot enter here, except to say that some of them were apparently young at the time they joined the group, or were exceptionally hardy and long-lived, since at least seven of the original members were still alive in the 1160s.

During its early years the group went through various changes, including a move to a new location and the departure of several members. Some of those who remained urged Geoffrey, who was called "master" and "the first hermit," that "They should transfer themselves and their place to some order," but he refused to give an answer. In 1134, however, when he was very ill, they proposed four alternatives: the black monks of Bonneval or Marmoutiers, the regular canons, or the abbey of Savigny, which they called "a famous monastery from which many monasteries have already been founded . . . and where the [monastic] order flowers again and whose sweet reputation is diffused everywhere."[64] To this Geoffrey replied, "Send if you wish to send." So Fontaines joined the order of Savigny (and later of Cîteaux, when Savigny became Cistercian), and bishop Hildebert of Le Mans, the famous poet and letter-writer, blessed Odo of Savigny as abbot and twelve of the hermits as monks.

Master Geoffrey, however, together with Geoffrey *Bullonus*, Ascelin, and many others, Peregrinus wrote, were unwilling to become monks, and they were allowed "to go wherever they wanted and to possess for as long as they lived whatever they wanted in either possessions or other things." Master Geoffrey went to live in the forest of Aiguevive and died at Montrichard. Geoffrey *Bullonus* went with Ascelin to a hermitage at Lande, which was given him in 1140 by Reginald of Château-Renault and later, in about 1150, was given to Fontaines as a grange by the bishop of Chartres at the request of Bernard of Clairvaux and others. In the meantime, Ascelin died, and Geoffrey *Bullonus* before his death gave himself and his possessions (which as a hermit he was allowed to own) to Fontaines and was buried there in the monks' cloister.[65]

The early history of Obazine, the third example of institutionalization that I shall discuss, is told in the *Life* of the founder, Stephen, of which the first book was written about 1166 and the second and third about 1180. When he was a young priest, Stephen wanted to renounce the world and sought the advice of the abbot of La Chaise-Dieu, who urged him not to delay his conversion. Together with another priest named Peter, therefore, he took "the habit of holy religion," and "freed from the ties of this world they entered the way of salvation with a free and unconditional step." After spending ten months with a hermit named Bertrand, who agreed that they could leave when they wanted "free and without complaint," they settled in about 1120 at Obazine, where they were joined by a cleric named Bernard. With the permission of the bishop of Limoges, they built a monastery where they followed, according to the *Life*, "the canonical rule in their liturgy and the heremitical life in their undertaking (*propositum*)." Stephen especially insisted that his followers, unlike many canons, who ate well and rested between the offices, must work with their hands for the whole day apart from the time spent in prayers and reading.[66]

The community grew rapidly. According to Stephen's *Life,* "Nobles and non-nobles, men no less than women, began to flock to the monastery from all sides and to submit their gentle necks to the sweet yoke of Christ." The men and women lived close together, the *Life* said, "separated in their dwelling but joined in religion." One nobleman came with his wife and children, his male and female retainers, and all his household goods, animals, and flocks. The fortifications of his former house were torn down, and it was turned into a monastery, and he himself became a monk and later a priest.[67] Although Stephen feared the cares of governing so many people and longed for the solitude "in which he could more privately and freely be quiet (*vacare*) for God and crucify his flesh with less restraint," he nevertheless embarked on building a new monastery, and reluctantly accepted the position of prior. He still maintained strict discipline, but less strict than when his followers had been "both fewer in numbers and more perfect in life." His word was law, since they followed "no established law of any order," and he taught only humility, obedience, poverty, discipline, and above all love. But "since the days of man are brief," wrote the author of Stephen's *Life,* "and human teachings (*humana magisteria*) flourish only as long as the preceptor is living or present, he wanted them to assume the profession of one of the orders authorized by the church, so that when there were no masters they would still have the continuous authority of a written law."[68] In the early 1130s they consulted the prior of La Chartreuse, who advised them to join the Cistercians,[69] but they continued to live without a written law and to follow Stephen's regulations, hesitating between becoming monks or canons, until finally, in 1142, they sent to the nearby abbey of Dalon for monks to teach them the monastic order. Stephen became a monk and abbot; the clerical brothers became monks; the non-clerical brothers, lay brothers; and the women, nuns, who were henceforth subject to strict enclosure.

This venture was not a success. The new monks of Obazine were experienced hermits but untrained in monastic life, and they disliked the ways imposed upon them by the monks of Dalon, who were hard masters and made no effort to lead the new monks slowly from their previous way of life to the unaccustomed rules.

"They demanded from them indiscriminately," according to the *Life*, "the entire observance of the monastic discipline and immediately disturbed, corrected, and censured them, both in the church and in other places." Stephen did his best to console and encourage his monks when they complained to him, but he did not interfere. When in 1147 Obazine finally broke away from Dalon and joined the order of Cîteaux, however, he specified "that everything that was contrary to the order would be slowly abolished lest the house could not bear a sudden change while it was still new." The Cistercian instructors proved to be more suitable than those from Dalon,[70] and this time the change was successful, but the previous problems illustrate the difficulty of transferring from a *humana magisteria* exercised by a charismatic leader with a distinctive view of religious life to a rule of written law imposed in an impersonal manner.

Similar difficulties are found in modern communities. Some time ago I spent a few days at St. Louis Priory, which was established in 1955 as a dependency of Ampleforth, in the north of England, from where the first monks came and where the early recruits were sent for their novitiate. But only two of them remained in monastic life. Some were unsuited from the beginning, according to the history of the priory published in 1980,

> others were deterred by the very difficult conditions and the difference in culture of the rather old-fashioned English monastic regime and personnel at Ampleforth. It was perhaps not sufficiently observed that these young recruits were not even English in origin. It is probable also that a number of would-be postulants were deterred by the prospect of a bleak novitiate in the damp uplands of the Yorkshire Moors when they might try somewhere else in the centrally heated United States. It is also clear that not all the authorities at Ampleforth understood the young Americans, and it is quite certain that the young Americans found it extremely difficult to understand the rather cold ways of the English.[71]

This passage could almost have been written, *mutatis mutandis*, about Obazine and Dalon in the early 1140s, when the new monks of Obazine, who were used to the freedom of eremitical life and the paternal, though ascetic, rule of Stephen, were faced with the strict and inflexible discipline of the monks of Dalon, who were supported by both authority and tradition. This type of tension was particularly prevalent in communities in the eleventh and twelfth centuries because at no other time in the history of monasticism, except perhaps at its origins, were so many people inspired by charismatic and often idiosyncratic religious leaders to seek a life devoted to the service of God. In doing so they faced a series of personal and later of collective decisions, starting with the determination to leave the secular world and often ending with the choice of some organized form of religious life. Not all of them, however, were willing to subject themselves to a rule and a superior, and some preferred to leave their former companions and seek a new home in the wilderness.

Historians tend to study communities that survived and left some records and to forget that many died out without a trace. For them, success is identified with continuity and growth and failure with decline and disappearance. It has been said that in religion nothing fails like success, or, presumably, succeeds like failure, but it is important to distinguish between different types of success and failure. Organization and growth were not failure, but they involved change. Refusal to organize was also not failure, even if it led to the end of the community. Some hermits gave up owing to the harshness of the life, and some communities died out owing to desertions, poverty, and hostility. Others disappeared when they had fulfilled their purpose. It was no failure for people to leave when the nature and purpose of the group changed and no longer met their religious needs. There was an intrinsically ephemeral element in the aspirations and vision of many of these men and women, and the only way to honor their commitment was to reject institutionalization and to start again, like Dado of Conques, Bernard of Tiron, and Geoffrey of Fontaines and his companions, who went to new hermitages when Fontaines became an abbey.[72] There is a touch of pride as well as of sadness in the words of abbot Peregrinus in his history of Fontaines when he wrote, after recording the reconciliation of Geoffrey *Bullonus* with the monks and his death and burial in the cloister, that "This was the end of the hermits."[73] It was indeed the end of the founding fathers of Fontaines, but not of their ideal of a life dedicated to the service of God in their own way.

Notes

CC:CM = Corpus Christianorum: Continuatio mediaeualis
JL = Philipp Jaffé, *Regesta pontificum Romanorum*, 2nd ed. (Leipzig, 1885–88)
PL = *Patrologia latina*

1. Colomban Bock, *La promesse d'obéissance ou la "Professio regularis"* (Westmalle, 1955), and Catherine Capelle, *Le voeu d'obéissance des origines au XIIe siècle*, doctoral dissertation, University of Strasbourg (Paris, 1959).

2. *Regula Magistri*, 89.11, ed. Adalbert de Vogüé, Sources chrétiennes 105–107 (Paris, 1964–65), II, 372; *Regula Benedicti*, 58.

3. Cassian, *Conlationes*, 19.5 and 21.24, ed. E. Pichery, Sources chrétiennes 42, 54, and 64 (Paris, 1955–59), III, 42–44 and 111.

4. *Regula Benedicti*, 59, and *The Rule of St. Benedict in Latin and English with Notes*, ed. Timothy Fry (Collegeville, Minn., 1981), 270–71. On the parallel between baptism and entry to religious life, see Giles Constable, "The Ceremonies and Symbolism of Entering Religious Life and Taking the Monastic Habit, from the Fourth to the Twelfth Century," in *Segni e riti nella chiesa altomedievale occidentale*, Settimane di studio del Centro italiano di studi sull'Alto Medioevo 33 (Spoleto, 1987), 779–80 and 799–800 and works cited there.

5. See Giles Constable, "Liberty and Free Choice in Monastic Thought and Life, especially in the Eleventh and Twelfth Centuries," in *La notion de liberté au moyen âge: Islam, Byzance, Occident*, ed. George Makdisi, Dominique Sourdel, and Janine Sourdel-Thomine, Penn-Paris-Dumbarton Oaks Colloquia 4 (Paris, 1985), 99–118.

6. *Cartulaire de l'abbaye cardinale de la Trinité de Vendôme*, ed. Charles Métais (Paris-Vendôme, 1893–1904), I, 335, no. 201. There is a parallel passage in the following charter, ibid., I, 336, no. 202.

7. Roger Baron, "L'idée de liberté chez S. Anselme et Hugues de Saint-Victor," *Recherches de théologie ancienne et médiévale* 32 (1965): 118–19.

8. Abelard, *Sermo 33 de Joanne Baptista*, in *PL*, CLXXVIII, 582BC.

9. Peter of Blois, *Ep.* 54, ed. J. A. Giles, Patres ecclesiae anglicanae (Oxford, 1847), I, 162–63.

10. Guibert of Nogent, *De vita sua*, I, 14, ed. Georges Bourgin, Collection de textes pour servir à l'étude et à l'enseignement de l'histoire 40 (Paris, 1907), 49–51.

11. Anselm, *Ep.* 168, ed. F. S. Schmitt (Edinburgh, 1946–61), IV, 44–45, dating this letter after Anselm's consecration as archbishop in 1093.

12. Ivo of Chartres, *Ep.* 41, ed. Jean Leclercq, Classiques de l'histoire de France au moyen âge 22 (Paris, 1949), 164–66, dating this letter 1094.

13. *Regula Benedicti*, 58.

14. Ambrose Wathen, "*Conversatio* and Stability in the Rule of Benedict," *Monastic Studies* 11 (1975): 1–44; *Rule of St. Benedict*, ed. Fry, 459–65; and Constable, "Ceremonies" (n. 4), 784–85.

15. *Regula Benedicti*, 61 and 73. See Adrian Hastings, "St. Benedict and the Eremitical Life," *Downside Review* 68 (1950): 191–211, and other works cited by Gregorio Penco, "Gli studi degli ultimi trent'anni intorno alla spiritualità della Regola di S. Benedetto," in *Probemi e orientamenti di spiritualità monastica, biblica e liturgica* (Rome, 1961), 218.

16. Albert, *Vita Guilielmi magni*, 4, ed. Guillaume de Waha (Liège, 1693), 401. See Kaspar Elm, *Beiträge zur Geschichte des Wilhelmitenordens*, Müntersche Forschungen 14 (Cologne-Graz, 1962), 26.

17. Herbert Grundmann, "Zur Vita s. Gerlaci eremitae," *Deutsches Archiv* 18 (1962): 541–43.

18. Peter Damiani, *Vita beati Romualdi*, 24, ed. Giovanni Tabacco, Fonti per la storia d'Italia 94 (Rome, 1957), 51; Ivo of Chartres, *Ep.* 256, in *PL*, CLXII, 261C.

19. See, for instance, Bernard of Clairvaux, *Serm.* 3 *in circumcisione*, 6, ed. Jean Leclercq et al. (Rome, 1957–77), IV, 286–87, and Joseph Grillon, "Bernard et les ermites et groupements érémitiques," in *Bernard de Clairvaux*, Commission d'histoire de l'ordre de Cîteaux 3 (Paris, 1953), 261–62.

20. Anselm, *Ep.* 37, ed. F. S. Schmitt (n. 11), III, 140; also in Eadmer, *Vita sancti Anselmi*, I, 20, ed. Richard W. Southern, Medieval Texts (London-Edinburgh, 1962), 33. See Richard W. Southern, *Saint Anselm and His Biographer* (Cambridge, 1963), 349.

21. Eadmer, *Vita Anselmi*, II, 11, ed. Southern (n. 20), 76.

22. Horst Fuhrmann, *Papst Urban II. und der Stand der Regularkanoniker*, Bayerische Akademie der Wissenschaften, Phil.-hist. Kl., Sitzungsberichte 1984.2 (Munich, 1984), 42–43.

23. Privilege for St-Gilles (1110/17), in *PL*, CLXIII, 416CD; JL 6540.

24. Jean Leclercq and Pierre Doyère, "Sur le statut des ermites monastiques," *La vie spirituelle. Supplément* XIV, 58 (1961): 384–403; Jacques Dubois, "La vie des moines dans les prieurés du moyen âge," *Lettre de Ligugé* 133 (1969): 10–33; and Benedicta Ward, "The Relationship between Hermits and Communities in the West, with special reference to the twelfth century," in *Solitude and Communion: Papers on the Hermit Life Given at St David's, Wales in the Autumn of 1975*, ed. A. M. Allchin, Fairacres Publications 66 (Oxford, 1977): 54–63.

25. Eadmer, *Vita sancti Oswaldi*, 5, in *The Historians of the Church of York and Its Archbishops*, ed. James Raine, Rolls Series 7 (London, 1879–94), II, 8–9.

26. Ordericus Vitalis, *Historia ecclesiastica*, 3, ed. Marjorie Chibnall, Oxford Medieval Texts (Oxford, 1969–80), III, 76.

27. Peter Damiani, *De gallica profectione*, 12, in *PL*, CXLV, 873CD.

28. Idem, *Ep.* VI, 5, in *PL*, CXLIV, 380AB.

29. Eadmer, *Vita Anselmi*, I, 5, ed. Southern (n. 20), 9. See Patrice Cousin, "Les relations de saint Anselme avec Cluny," in *Spicilegium Beccense*, 1. *Congrès international du IXe centenaire de l'arrivée d'Anselme au Bec* (Le Bec-Hellouin-Paris, 1959), 438–39 and 452, where he dated this episode 1057/9, and Southern, *Anselm* (n. 20), 28.

30. Peter Damiani, *Ep.* VI, 3, in *PL*, CXLIV, 373C.

31. John of Salerno, *Vita sancti Odonis*, I, 25 and 28, in *PL*, CXXXIII, 54C and 55C.

32. Kenneth John Conant, *Cluny. Les églises et la maison du chef d'ordre*, Mediaeval Academy of America, Publ. 77 (Mâcon, 1968), 50.

33. *Recueil des chartes de l'abbaye de Cluny*, ed. Auguste Bernard and Alexandre Bruel, Collection de documents inédits sur l'histoire de France (Paris, 1876–1903), IV, 801–803, no. 3633.

34. Walter, *Vita sancti Anastasii*, in *PL*, CXLIX, 425–32 (quotes on 428C and 428D–9A), and *Vita sancti Morandi*, in *Bibliotheca Cluniacensis*, ed. Martin Marrier and André Duchesne (Paris, 1614), 501–506 (quote on 506AB). See Paolo Lamma, *Momenti di storiografia Cluniacense*, Istituto storico italiano per il Medio Evo: Studi storici 42–44 (Rome, 1961), 72–73, and Noreen Hunt, *Cluny under Saint Hugh 1049–1109* (London, 1967), 87.

35. *Vita beati Gaufredi Castaliensis*, I, 1, ed. A. Bosvieux, in *Mémoires de la société des sciences naturelles et archéologiques de la Creuse* 3 (1862): 79.

36. Peter the Venerable, *De miraculis*, I, 8, in *CC:CM*, LXXXIII, 30–31, and *Ep.* 58, ed. Giles Constable, Harvard Historical Studies 78 (Cambridge, Mass., 1967), I, 162, and II, 134–35. On eremitism at Cluny in the twelfth century, see Jean Leclercq, "Pierre le Vénérable et l'érémitisme clunisien," in *Petrus Venerabilis 1156–1956: Studies and Texts Commemorating the Eighth Centenary of His Death*, ed. Giles Constable and James Kritzeck, Studia Anselmiana 40 (Rome, 1956), 99–120, and Peter the Venerable, *Epp.* 123–29, ed. Constable, I, 317–27, and II, 182.

37. Jean Leclercq, "L'érémitisme et les Cisterciens," in *L'eremitismo in Occidente nei secoli XI e XII. Atti della seconda Settimana internazionale di studio: Mendola, 30 agosto–6 settembre 1962*, Pubblicazioni dell'Università cattolica del Sacro Cuore, Contributi, 3 S.: Varia 4, Miscellanea del centro di studi medioevali 4 (Milan, 1965), 575–76, and E. Mikkers in the discussion, esp. 579–80 on eremitical tendencies among the Cistercians.

38. Galland of Rigny, *Libellus proverbiorum*, 13, ed. Jean Chatillon, in *Revue du moyen âge latin* 9 (1953): 47, cf. 105.

39. Bernard of Clairvaux, *De gradibus humilitatis et superbiae*, 14, ed. Jean Leclercq (n. 19), III, 48–49, cf. trans. George B. Burch (Cambridge, Mass., 1940), 209.

40. *Decretales Gregorii IX*, IX, 31, 8 (JL 13854), in *Corpus iuris canonici*, ed. Emil Friedberg (Leipzig, 1879), II, 571.

41. *Vita venerabilis Amedaei Altae Ripae*, 2 and 5, ed. M.-Anselme Dimier, in *Studia monastica* 5 (1963): 273–78 and 284–88 (quotes on 284 and 288).

42. *Veterum scriptorum . . . amplissima collectio*, ed. Edmond Martène and Ursin Durand (Paris, 1724–33), I, 784A.

43. William of Wyecombe, *Vita Roberti Betun*, 12, in *Anglia sacra*, ed. Henry Wharton (London, 1691), II, 305–306.

44. Marbod of Rennes, *Ep.* 6, in *PL*, CLXXI, 1483CD, and with some differences, Johannes von Walter, *Die ersten Wanderprediger Frankreichs*, 1. *Robert von Arbrissel*, Studien zur Geschichte der Theologie und der Kirche IX, 3 (Leipzig, 1903), 186.

45. *Vitae s. Roberti Knaresburgensis*, ed. Paul Grosjean, *Analecta Bollandiana* 57 (1939): 370–72.

46. *Vita Stephani Muretensis*, 32, in *CC:CM*, VIII, 121–22.

47. Geoffrey Grossus, *Vita s. Bernardi Tironiensis*, in *PL*, CLXXII, 1367–446.

48. See Louis Gougaud, "La vie érémitique au moyen âge," *Revue d'ascétique et de mystique* 1 (1920): 209; Jean Leclercq, "La spiritualité des chanoines réguliers," in *La vita comune del clero nei secoli XI e XII. Atti della Settimana di studio: Mendola, settembre 1959*, Pubblicazioni dell'Università cattolica del Sacro Cuore, 3 S.: Scienze storiche 2–3, Miscellanea del centro di studi medioevali 3 (Milan, 1962), I, 134; Jean Becquet, "L'érémitisme clérical et laïc dans l'Ouest de la France," in *Eremitismo* (n. 37), 200–201; Henrietta Leyser, *Hermits and the New Monasticism* (London, 1984), 113–18, listing seventy-three houses with eremitical origins; and Brian Golding, *Gilbert of Sempringham and the Gilbertine Order c. 1130–c. 1300* (Oxford, 1995), 78–79.

49. *Libellus de diversis ordinibus et professionibus qui sunt in aecclesia*, ed. Giles Constable and Bernard Smith, Oxford Medieval Texts (Oxford, 1972), 14–16. See Ludo Milis, "Ermites et chanoines réguliers au XIIe siècle," *Cahiers de civilisation médiévale* 22 (1979): 61.

50. Gert Melville, "Zur Funktion der Schriftlichkeit im institutionellen Gefüge mittelalterlicher Orden," *Frühmittelalterliche Studien* 25 (1991): 391–417, and "'Diversa sunt monasteria et diversas habent institutiones'. Aspetti delle molteplici forme organizzative dei religiosi nel Medioevo," in *Chiesa e società in Sicilia. I secoli XII–XVI*, ed. G. Zito (Turin, 1995), 323–45, esp. 329.

51. IV Lateran, 13, in *Conciliorum oecumenicorum decreta*, ed. G. Alberigo et al., 3rd ed. (Bologna, 1973), 242.

52. Mary Douglas, *In the Wilderness: The Doctrine of Defilement in the Book of Numbers*, Journal for the Study of the Old Testament: Supplement Series 158 (Sheffield, 1993), 53.

53. See the typikon of Galesios, 223, in *Byzantine Monastic Foundation Documents*, ed. John Thomas and Angela Hero, Dumbarton Oaks Studies 35 (Washington, D.C., 2000), I, 163.

54. Jean Becquet, "Face à la mort dans les ordres nouveaux du Limousin," in *Moines et moniales face à la mort. Actes du colloque de Lille 2, 3 et 4 octobre 1992* (Paris-Lille, 1993), 72.

55. Hervé Oudart, "L'ermite et le prince. Les débuts de la vie monastique à Conques (fin VIIIᵉ–début IXᵉ siècle)," *Revue historique* 297 (1997): 36–38. For a somewhat different account of the origins of Conques, see the grant of Pepin I of Aquitaine in 838, in *Recueil des actes de Pépin Iᵉʳ et Pépin II rois d'Aquitaine (814–848)*, ed. Léon Levillain (Paris, 1926), 133–51, with a long introduction by the editor.

56. It is uncertain whether the "good monks" were outsiders, as I tend to believe, or insiders, as Oudart, "L'ermite et le prince" (n. 55), 18, proposed (translating *"per bonorum monachorum consultum"* as "by the resolution of the good monks"). According to Ardo, *Vita Benedicti abbatis Anianensis et Indensis*, 36, in *Monumenta germaniae historica, Scriptores* XV.1, 215, Louis the Pious sent inspectors to monasteries to make sure his orders were observed.

57. *Vita* [B] *Norberti*, IX, 50–51, in *PL*, CLXX, 1291B–2B, and ibid., X, 57, col. 1296C.

58. *Fundacio abbathie de Kyrkestall*, ed. E. K. Clark, in *Publications of the Thoresby Society*, IV: *Miscellanea* (Leeds, 1895), 177–78.

59. Giles Constable, *The Reformation of the Twelfth Century* (Cambridge, 1996), 123.

60. Charles Dereine, "La spiritualité 'apostolique' des premiers fondateurs d'Affligem (1083–1100)," *Revue d'histoire ecclésiastique* 54 (1959): 44, n. 2, cf. 52, n. 1.

61. *Annales Rodenses*, ed. P. C. Boeren and G. W. A. Panhuysen (Assen, 1968), 38 and 42.

62. *Gallia christiana*, II, instr. 491–92.

63. Peregrinus, *Historia monasterii beatae Mariae de Fontanis Albis*, in *Recueil des chroniques de Touraine*, ed. André Salmon, Société archéologique de Touraine, Collection de documents sur l'histoire de Touraine 1 (Tours, 1854), 257–91. Book I (258–73) is a narrative history, and Book II (273–91) is concerned with the liberties and possessions of the abbey and consists of two parts: one of five papal privileges and the other of thirteen other charters.

64. A similar situation arose at Silvanès, where "a great dispute" arose among the early members over which order to join, "with some praising the order of the Cistercians, others the Carthusians, and some saying that they should build a suitable monastery of virgin nuns": see Hugh of Silvanès, *Tractatus de conversione Pontii de Larazio et exordii Salvaniensis monasterii vera narratio*, 21, in Etienne Baluze, *Miscellanea*, ed. J.D. Mansi (Lucca, 1761–64), I, 183.

65. Peregrinus, *Historia* (n. 63), 284–85, for the grant of Reginald made in 1140 "after he [Geoffrey] separated himself from the society of the monks of Fontaines," and 286–87, for the grant of the bishop of Chartres.

66. *Vita s. Stephani Obazinensis*, I, 2 and 7, ed. Michel Aubrun, Publications de l'Institut d'études du Massif Central 6 (Clermont-Ferrand, 1970), 48 and 54.

67. Ibid., I, 29–30, ed. Aubrun (n. 66), 86 and 90.

68. Ibid., II, 1, ed. Aubrun (n. 66), 96.

69. The founder of Silvanès, Pontius of Laraze, likewise consulted the prior of La Chartreuse, who advised him to join the Cistercians (see n. 64). Pontius himself became a lay brother.

70. *Vita Stephani*, II, 7 and 12, ed. Aubrun (n. 66), 101 and 114.

71. *In the Lord's Service: Saint Louis Priory 1955/1980*, ed. Ralph Wright (n.p., n.d. [St. Louis, 1980]), 37–38.

72. The same may be true of the dissidents at Kirkstall and Chancelade, whose fate is unknown.

73. Peregrinus, *Historia* (n. 63), 265.

CHAPTER TWO

Visual Communities in Byzantium and Medieval Islam

Anthony Cutler

As I write these words, the cyrillic letter C (S in the roman alphabet) is being painted on doorposts in Kosovo. A fairly simple sign, it is still one that a newspaper's editors find necessary to explain to their readers.[1] At the lowest level within its store of meanings, it identifies the householders as Serbs, a long-recognized compound of ethnic, linguistic, and religious elements newly recharged by the force of recent events. That these are the constituents of a cultural community is indicated by the emblem's second level of signification: "C" refers to the alliteration "Samo sloga Srbina spasava"—only unity will save the Serbs—a slogan that in turn evokes a history at least as ancient as 1389 when, at Kosovo Polje, what was in fact a coalition of Serbs, Bosnians, and Albanians took on the Muslim army of Murad I. As a result, Serbia became a vassal state of the Ottomans, even while Serbian epics treat the battle as a moral victory and the foundation of subsequent resistance to the Turks.[2]

Alliterative affirmations of shared belief have a long history in Orthodox culture. Coded and thereby nominally exclusive, they operate by means of both abbreviation and allusion. Thus on the Esztergom *staurotheke,* a twelfth-century container for a fragment of the True Cross, the most prominent graphic elements are the four enameled medallions, each inscribed with a *chi* ($\bar{X}$) on a brilliant blue ground (Fig. 1). Flanking them in the upper quadrants are Constantine, whose vision of the Cross is held to have shaped Byzantium's Christian destiny, and his mother Helena, who is said to have discovered the Cross that testifies to the fragment's authenticity.[3] The imperial pair point to the relic, as a Jew does below, thereby identifying it with the wood on which Christ, standing beside him, died for our sins. To the right, the crucified is tenderly lowered. There is no depiction of his (or the beholder's) resurrection for none is needed. The work is described, the economy of salvation assured, by the encrypted acronym: *Christos charin christianois charizetai* (Christ gives [his] grace to the Christians). That this rebus was generally understood in the Middle Byzantine world argues for a chronologically and regionally restricted "grammar," one more limited than Chomsky's notion of the rules with which the human mind comes equipped and by means of which it constructs, understands, and ultimately transforms a finite set of terms into an unlimited number of sentences.[4] At the same time, the fact that at the beginning of the twenty-first century we need the four *chi*s explained to us before we can transform them into anything more meaningful than ornament shows that we are faced with a culturally circumscribed message: medieval Greek experience of the sign, in contrast to our unawareness, constrained what the Byzantines saw in it and allowed its conversion into a meaningful, and supposedly salvific, principle. It is clear that the sign per se does not determine this interpretation. A pre-existent community is required for its significance to be grasped.

Yet, at least in the case of the Esztergom reliquary, more than language is involved in the transformation. As we have seen, the *chi*s are enclosed within a sequence of images, as the wood is enfolded in a carapace of gilded silver and enamel. Only the medieval Christian who believed that the Jews were responsible for the death of Christ and that this death, in turn, created a community of grace; only the Byzantine who saw the emperor and empress of his or her own time in the archaic, heavily bejeweled forms labeled Constantine and Helena would know to convert these figures into a narrative that starts with death—the ascent of and descent from the Cross—and ends with the implication of eternal life. The process is teleological, but it is an active one, shaped by the Greek Christian mind and guided by a culturally defined system. A shared vision as much as a shared language determined the transformation imposed on these signs by the Byzantine eye.[5]

If, as I have tried to suggest, this process presupposes both a cognitive and creedal community it does not follow that its end result—the congeries of signs that make up that community's visual lexicon—was comprehensible only to its members. A Syriac Jewish writer of the thirteenth century, the physician Gregory Abū'l Faraj, repeatedly tells of battles against the Arabs waged by Greek and Frankish armies whose victory was symbolized, as he put it, by "the crosses of gold and silver on the heads of their spears."[6] To my knowledge no such battle crosses survive. Perhaps they were melted down for their precious-metal content, or it could be that processional crosses, of which a fair number are preserved and normally used in sacred and civic rituals, were pressed into military service—one example of the transformations that will be of concern to us below. The best known of these are elaborate examples in silver gilt,[7] perhaps of the sort illustrated in the Skylitzes Chronicle, shown borne through the city when the population of Constantinople turned out to pray for the end of a drought in 1037 (Fig. 2). Following the crosses and what would seem to be reliquaries borne by the emperor's brothers come two bishops followed at a distance by the "people." Despite the sardine-can arrangement of this last group and their exclusively male gender and brightly colored clothing, this twelfth-century vignette is sufficiently close to an eyewitness account of a procession formed to appease Providence after the earthquake that struck Edessa in Mesopotamia in 449 for us to recognize the *longue durée* of communal performance in the Christian East. On this occasion, the bishop Peter

> took all his clergy and all members of religious orders, both men and women, and all the lay members of the holy Church, both rich and poor, men, women and children, and they traversed all the streets of the city carrying crosses, with psalms and hymns, clad in the black garments of humility.[8]

Nonetheless, the inhabitants of the miniature display a segmentation more pronounced than that of the literary account. This articulation of the community, and in particular the division between churchmen and laity, finds its representation in architecture and decoration when, in and after the eleventh century, the *bema* (sanctuary) was separated from the nave of the church not only by a progressively more elaborate, icon-bearing screen but also by mosaics or painted images that constituted a program in its own right, distinct from that of the body of the church.[9] As if aware of such fragmentation, the Byzantines devised various schemes to restore at least a theoretical unity to the fellowship in Christ. In the liturgical hymn known as the Cheroubikon the faithful are temporarily incorporated into the ranks of the saints.[10] Conversely, holy men and bishops, in the form of "fictive icons" painted in the *bemas* of churches, suggest that these saints were part of the population of worshippers.[11] It is only superficially a paradox that, after Iconoclasm, when differentiation between the sacred and the profane came evermore to characterize Greek society, one of the functions attributed to works of art was the illusion that they and their beholders formed an ideal, uniform community. The difference between this posture and the mission assigned to images in the fifth century is marked. Then, as if to register a gulf that could be bridged only by intense moral effort, Neilos, abbot of Sinai, expressed the hope that ordinary people might "by gazing at pictures, become mindful of the manly deeds of those of us who have genuinely served the true God and . . . be forced to emulate those glorious and celebrated feats."[12] In the concerns of theologians and in practice this collective attitude was increasingly replaced by one that dictated the relationship between the individual and the icon that he or she venerated.[13]

Like all processual developments this change was marked by no single dramatic event; indeed, many of the older ways in which religious activity had been promoted persisted well into the Middle Ages. The communal sponsorship of church building and decoration, widespread in early Byzantium,[14] occurred as late as 1052 when a bishop Leo, Niketas, *protospatharios* and *tourmarches* of Naxia, and Stephanos, count and *kamelares*, identified themselves on the screen that once divided the nave from the *bema* of a church on the island of Naxos as those responsible for its restoration.[15] Ancient Gospel stories lived on as in an eleventh-century icon at Mount Sinai (Fig. 3) where the events of Christ's infancy culminate in a scene of the Massacre of the Innocents that departs little from the sixth-century accounts of John of Ephesus of the devastation caused by Justinian's legions in Persia:

> the Romans [as John calls them], in impious sport, went so far as to seize hold of the little children of one or two years of age,

and, taking them by one leg, and another by the other, threw them as high in the air as they could, and then caught them as they fell on their spears and swords and, running them through, cast them to the dogs.[16]

It is possible that John's description was itself affected by a picture that he had seen. But whether or not this was so, the mutual reinforcement of art and experience remained a powerful agent in the compact between spectators and the work of the image-makers they encountered or employed. This bond is more central to an understanding of the meaning that artistic production had for its original audience than the exegesis that characterizes most art-historical commentary. Thus the Crucifixion, typically shown raised above a skull, is all too often explained as occurring at Golgotha, a toponym signifying in Hebrew the place of the skull (*sc.* Adam's), as if ordinary Greeks knew that language and would have been moved more by this scholarly nicety than by the emblem's role as a *memento mori*, an index to the relation between Christ's death and their own noted above, or, at the very least, a reminder of things evident in a village cemetery after a heavy storm. So, too, of the scene of his Baptism (Fig. 4)—the archetype of Christian initiation into the community—we are told that the old man who often appears in the stream is a personification of the Jordan, derived from Roman images of river gods; while the youths undressing beside or swimming in the river are frequently read either as references to others whom John had baptized or as genre details, trivial attendants intended to lend a dose of realism to the scene. At one level such explanations contain a kernel of truth, but this sort of analysis emphasizes exactly the wrong thing—the origin, rather than the significance, of particulars. Perhaps one Byzantine in ten thousand would have known of the river gods that figure in pagan art. But ninety-nine out of one hundred, confronted with the detail of the swimming boys, would have immediately thought of what happens, and happens to this day in Greece, when on 6 January the priest blesses the waters in commemoration of the Epiphany and a host of hardy youth plunges into the sea or the stream that courses through their mountains, in celebration of the event.[17]

To dismiss as insignificant, or to neutralize an image by means of excessive erudition, is a decision made in the modern mind, not in the visual intelligence of those who first saw such pictures. It likewise has the unfortunate effect of imposing a purely "spiritual" content upon Byzantine art and thus of divorcing it from the "secular" interests of contemporaneous Islam, allegedly preoccupied with a world of earthly pleasures in its depictions of drinking, dancers, musicians, and scenes from everyday life.[18] To regard Arab communities as devoted merely to things of the flesh is a peculiar form of orientalism beyond the confines of this essay. But the corollary approach to Byzantine artifacts, treating them only as expressions of antiquarian or immaterial concern is scarcely less misleading. Thus many aspects of a magnificent Orthodox paten (Fig. 5)—a plate on which the eucharistic bread is served— echo the interests of Arab writers in material splendor. Assembled in such later collections as the *Book of Gifts and Rarities*,[19] these reports lovingly dwell on the precious and semi-precious stones, gilding and other decoration applied to objects, but regard these as demonstrations of generosity and/or politically driven largesse. Were it not for its central enameled image, the gem-encrusted plate in question could be a masterwork of Islamic art. On the other hand, this very scene can be seen to function in terms of the cognitive system set out above. Scholarly commentary tells us that the apostles sit around a sigma-shaped table, "an Early Christian tradition," and that the fish in their midst is there because in Greek this word was understood as an acronym for "Jesus Christ, Son of God, Savior."[20] Both observations are correct, but hardly useful, implying as they do that those who received bread from it were more interested in antiquarian lore and philology than in eternal life. More to the point is that these consumers—for this in all senses is what they were—saw themselves as actually participating in the Lord's supper by taking and eating a portion of his body.

Many patens are inscribed with Christ's words on the occasion of the Eucharist's institution (Matt. 26:26). These serve as instructions on the way in which membership in the community can be attained. In both Orthodox and Muslim belief systems this company is limited neither by space nor time: it matters little where one takes communion or participates in Friday prayer. And when one does, the company of observers includes those who lived a long time ago, those whose absence is negated by their likenesses, as in the case of the bishops of Christian antiquity present in the apses of churches (Fig. 6), and by the scrolls that they hold, usually consisting of prayers associated with the rite that the bishops concelebrate.[21] These texts could normally be read only by the clergy—a community within the community—with privileged access to the *bema*. But visible to all Muslims, and functionally equivalent, was the word of God as set out in the Koran and deployed in mosques like the Dome of the Rock (Fig. 7). Above the mosaic's paradisal imagery inscriptions display not only the proclamations of Allah but points of dogma such as a condemnation of supposed Christian polytheism.[22] In one instance the decoration was temporally extended when the caliph al-Ma'mūn (813–833) substituted his name for that of the Ummayad 'Abd al-Malik (685–705), the mosque's founder. More than a sign of *prise de possession*,[23] the later 'Abbasid ruler hereby associated himself with the declarations of belief that precede and follow his claim, implicitly joining the ranks of Muslim prophets, saints, and martyrs— in short, the Islamic *'ummah* (community).

Al-Ma'mūn was the first caliph to impose himself on the Dome of the Rock in this way, but by no means the first to appropriate the material splendor of the monument to serve his own ends. Already between 705 and 715 al-Walīd, the son of 'Abd al-Malik, had undertaken to construct or reconstruct the four major mosques of the Muslim world, treating as paradigmatic the Dome's gold and glass mosaics. Despite this reference, the reception enjoyed by this traditionally Byzantine medium in the Prophet's mosque at Medīna says much about the nexus between forms of decoration and religious identity. When he asked the son of the third caliph who had built the mosque what he thought of the reconstruction, al-Walīd received the reply "We built it in the manner of mosques, you built it in the manner of churches."[24]

The very fact that this response is recorded is some measure of the extent to which the caliph was regarded as the protector of true belief, and as the exemplar of conduct supposed to embody this role. Particularly after the end of Iconoclasm, when the defenders of images sought to paint the emperors who had strayed from Orthodoxy as contemptible heretics, the behavior of rulers of the Byzantine state was no less attentively scrutinized. It was not enough to allow holy icons or even to sponsor their creation. They must be embraced[25] and fought for, as is made clear by a miniature in the Skylitzes manuscript that we have already considered. By way of epitomizing the triumphant return of John I Tzimiskes from a campaign in Bulgaria, the painter shows the emperor at the head of his army but behind a car bearing an icon of the Mother of God (Fig. 8). The order of precedence is much as in the drought picture (Fig. 2), but instead of the cross, a generic sign of Christian faith, imperial devotion is focused upon an icon turned toward the beholder of both of the procession and the picture that illustrates the event. Byzantinists have long abandoned the attempt to identify a specific "type" of the Virgin and Child with the labels—Hodegetria, Eleousa, Glykophilousa, and so on—reported in literary sources and sometimes inscribed on surviving images. Suffice it to describe the icon that precedes John as a half-length version of the Mother with her cheek close to that of her son. Over time, this disposition enjoyed almost infinite variety, a precondition perhaps of its persistence: it remains an essential and enduring focus of devotion wherever Orthodox communities are found. For example, despite the crowns that they wear and the fact that Mary supports Jesus on her left arm rather than her right as in the miniature, it is found on an Ethiopian icon now in Santa Fe, New Mexico, made about 1960 (Fig. 9). The Amharic description identifies the Child as the Lamb, a biblical epithet (John 1:29) elaborated and made all the more poignant by the fact that the object is woven in wool.

Less important than the probability that a wood panel was the support of the icon in the miniature is the emphasis on the emperor, shown crowned and riding a white horse. As has already been pointed out, one of the major concerns of post-Iconoclastic ideologues was the imperial attitude toward icons. The ninth-century *Life* of St. Irene of Chrysobalanton, a legendary figure of unspecified date, tells the story of an apparition that visited an (unidentified) emperor, claiming to be the holy woman. To verify the vision, the ruler ordered an artist to represent her. (Needless to say, the experiment produced a positive result).[26] The story demonstrates the importance attached to the painted likenesses of saints and the role that visionary experience played in fortifying shared beliefs. From an early date men and women corroborated their visions by means of the aspects of saints familiar from works of art. This transference is made explicit in the early seventh century when pilgrims to the ciborium of St. Demetrios in Thessalonike identified the saint by "the costume that he wore on his icons."[27] Epiphanies of this sort might change their clothes — Demetrios appeared to some in a white mantle "like a consul," to others dressed as a soldier on the walls of the city during the Avar-Sklavene siege of the city in 586.[28] Even so, their potency was invariably guaranteed by the fact that they were recognizable. Little wonder, then, that by this time icons had assumed the might of the relics that emperors sought as helpmeets in war.[29]

Tests of the extent to which such faith was a communal sentiment include the social range across which it was manifested and the mechanism by which it was diffused. Even if we ignore the numbers in which they survive as *a priori* evidence for the popularity they enjoyed, icons perform highly on both counts. Pankratios of Taormina is said to have defended his city with the aid of images,[30] a tale promulgated in the early eighth-century *vita* of this fictitious saint, while the healing of a deaf-mute Jewish girl by the Virgin and St. Demetrios, whom she identified via their icons in a baptistery, serves as the springboard for a sermon of the famous ninth-century savant known as Leo the Mathematician.[31] Their reputation advertised in hagiography and homiletic, icons were both an instrument and a proof of communal cohesion, qualities that could only intensify as Byzantine society came under attack from the force that would eventually overwhelm it. A chronicler hostile to the Ottoman cause relates that the sultan Orhan, after capturing Nicaea in 1331, sent a commercial mission to Constantinople to sell the many icons, manuscripts, and relics that he had taken in the city. In light of what we have seen above, there can be little doubt that the Muslim leader knew a ready market when he saw one.

Awareness in Islam of Orthodox devotion to Christian shrines and artifacts was nothing new. This attachment was especially keen when the faithful lived *in partibus infidelibus*, as the Spanish traveler Ibn al-Zubayr noted when he visited Damascus in 1184:

Inside the city is a church held in great consideration by the Rum. It is called Mary's Church, and after the temple in Jerusalem they have none more esteemed than this. It is an elegant structure with remarkable pictures that amaze the mind and hold the gaze and its spectacle is wonderful indeed. It is in the hands of the Rum, who are never molested within it.[32]

If a Muslim could so react to Christian images the response of those who sponsored them or worshipped in their midst is hardly surprising. More than piety was at work here: the faithful merged with the universe of the living and the dead by paying for pictures that would be publicly exposed. On these they imposed their votive statements or placed beside them dedicatory statements, as a woman named Kyriake did next to the image of her name-saint in a church at Upper Bouliarioi in the Peloponnese.[33] Pictures inscribed in this way are less often noted[34] than those in which the donor had himself or herself physically represented, but they are more widespread and evidence of no less devotion. Depictions of saints and those who paid for them are famously absent from Islamic art, but the liturgies of congregational mosques provided, and still provide, occasion for the inclusion of names of the elect, rulers and other worthies, in the *khutba*, the sermon pronounced on Fridays and during great festivals. Like inscriptions, these were verbal signs denoting membership in the community; to be mentioned no longer was to be cast out, a political strategy frequently resorted to by the founders and would-be founders of new dynasties.[35] In the Christian world, images could similarly be expunged. When, in the second quarter of the fourteenth century, the convent of Maroules was converted into a male monastery, the female saints on the walls of the church were replaced by figures of monks.[36]

Yet it would be a mistake to confine the notion of visual and verbal communities to rites celebrated in monastic or ecclesiastical arenas. Already in the eleventh century, the *Life* of St. Mary the Younger treats her devotion to an icon of the Mother of God, before which she prostrated herself at home, as an acceptable alternative to attendance at church,[37] clearly an attitude that recognized a *fait accompli*. But the substitution implies no diminished sense of creedal identity. The reverence for icons, either in domestic chapels[38] or on a purely individual basis, reinforced rather than replaced the ties that bound one believer to another. If the survival rates of small panels accurately express an incremental growth in their production in and after the twelfth century, we can infer a vast increase in private devotion. Many of these are labeled as the Hodegetria or similar epithets, associating them with major works in public and monastic shrines. Further filiations of this sort are apparent on reliquaries and *enkolpia*, amulets worn around the neck that served to mark the wearer's faith in, and attachment to, saints often highly regarded for their apotropaic powers. Thus Michael Italikos, in the second half of the twelfth century, sent as a gift to a friend who had become a doctor an *enkolpion* consisting of a coin that depicted Constantine the Great and Helena, saints who in popular belief protected the bearer from plague.[39] This is a minor but interesting example since Michael was a philosopher who served as a sort of counselor to the physicians of Constantinople. The capital had long since seen the gradual sacralization of its worldly rituals. In the tenth-century *Book of the Eparch* candidates for the office of notary, after taking an oath before the city prefect, are required to "go to the church nearest their residence" and, after removing their secular garments, don a white chasuble (*phelonion*) and be blessed by a priest. The newly appointed figure is then required to carry a Bible while the *primikerios* (in this case the holder of a priestly office) holds a censer the fumes of which he directs toward the notary. The character of the ceremony is made plain by the anonymous author's symbolizing mindset: the candidate's ways, he says, "shall be made straight as the incense [which ascends] before the face of the Lord."[40]

At least when we have texts, sub-groups such as doctors and lawyers within the Christian populations are easier to detect than looser associations seemingly based only on faith. Indeed we are often dependent on written records to flesh out the significance of objects of which at most one or two examples exist. For instance, it is primarily in the light of such texts as the *Miracula* of St. Demetrios, cited above, that we can penetrate the secret of a hinged *enkolpion* in the British Museum (Fig. 10), of which the front lid is missing. The enamel on its back cover shows a half-length St. George surrounded by the legend "He supplicates you to be his fervent guardian in battles." This is a sentiment perfectly appropriate to the warrior saint. But the text that runs around the medallion—"Being anointed by your blood and your myrrh"—is not.[41] Not until the object is opened, the prone body concealed beneath a rectangular flap (Fig. 11) observed, and this compared to written descriptions of the ciborium of St. Demetrios, is the object's relation to the saint's shrine in Thessalonike made clear. Up to this point we have discovered no more than the means to associate the amulet with a broadly based city cult.[42] But the existence of a similar *enkolpion*, inscribed with the name of its owner

(Sergios), again mentioning the blood and myrrh of Demetrios and two other "victorious martyrs" (Sergios and Bakchos) and an invocation to the saint to protect the wearer both in life and death,[43] allows us to infer a group of artifacts favored by the military élite, a group restricted even more by its calling and its wealth—both pieces are decorated in cloisonné enamel on gold—than by its faith.

The way to a more precise definition of the class for which such amulets were made lies in our ability to perceive the well-defined rules that governed their production. Their meaning, for us as well as for their original clientèle, depends upon information that is gathered by the retina but processed by the mind. Both the rules and their application are expressions of the primary cognitive community to which we seek access. At the same time, it is clear that the rules of representation could vary according to the ends that such objects were made to serve. The Demetrios *enkolpia* present a specific, if at first cryptic, body of information that requires of the modern beholder a fairly sophisticated awareness of the circumstances of their creation. Less specific, indeed deliberately more generic, is the content of an icon such as the thirteenth-century panel in Athens depicting St. George framed by a partially destroyed sequence of scenes from his life (Fig. 12). In contrast to the particularities of Demetrios' interment and the architectural setting that afforded entrée to the devout who desired the holy fluids available at his ciborium, the vignettes surrounding George, while adhering to popular narratives about him—his renunciation of wealth, his interrogation by a secular ruler, the tortures and death he undergoes—are constants of a martyr's *curriculum vitae*, the stuff of hagiography and, to some extent, of the life of Christ. They call up analogies in the beholder's mind and by this means broaden rather than narrow the audience to whom the picture appealed.

The objectives of this generic design may be related to its frequently noted "hybrid" character.[44] This term has been applied not, as some might suppose, because the double-sided icon combines the figure of the saint raised in wood relief with the traditional painted panel, but on account of features said to be characteristic of Italian retables employed alongside the Byzantine attitude of prostration in which the picture's (Western) donor is represented. Accordingly, a variety of places of origin—among them Cyprus and the Latin Kingdom of Jerusalem—have been mooted.[45]

One implication of such propositions is that the icon could not have issued from a self-consciously homogeneous community. No doubt Byzantine art sought to project an image of unity, distinguishing itself from the ethnicity and cultures of other peoples. Thus, famously, in the David and Goliath page of the Paris Psalter (MS Bibliothèque Nationale, gr. 139), the troops of the latter, following the Septugint text, are labeled *allophyloi* (other tribes) in contradistinction to the Israelites.[46] But the fantasy of cultural if not racial homogeneity is exposed in Byzantine literature itself. For example, the Thessalonican visions of St. Demetrios with which we have been concerned above include his apparition walking on the waters of the Aegean, a vision that the text says was vouchsafed also to the Jews of the city.[47] As to material possessions, if the occasional Islamic plate is held to be an alien incursion,[48] the epic known as the *Digenis Akritis* shows the extent to which a Greek border-warrior was ready to employ the artifacts of a culture that had been scorned for centuries in Byzantine religious polemic. Beyond the numerous turbans and caftans worn by the characters in the poem, its eponymous hero receives from his father, in addition to enameled icons of St. Theodore, "two Arab spears of young wood." Later in the poem a similar weapon is wielded by the Amazon Maximou with whom Digenis commits adultery.[49]

There is of course no reason why, in the Middle Ages any more than today, an object identified as of Arab origin should not have been made or used by a Christian. To insist otherwise would be to subscribe to the myth of *Ellenismos,* the romantic notion that "Greekness" and Orthodoxy were synonymous concepts. In contrast, a well-known and typical eleventh-century miniature shows the hermit Symeon the Stylite on his column in Syria revered not only by a Byzantine monk but also by what is obviously a group of Arabs (Fig. 13). Still, Christian Greek historians and theologians sought to repel the alien, a concept founded as much on historical geography as on religious practice and belief. Thus, according to a later chronicler, when the emperor Heraclius recaptured the True Cross from the Arabs, it was shown to Modestos, the Patriarch of Jerusalem (628–631), who observed that since the seal of its container was unbroken the relic was "untouched by the profane and murderous hands of the barbarians and unseen by them."[50] Intactness, purity, were evidently conditions of the power of the cross, as is made clear by John of Rhodes who speaks of Constantine the

Great defeating "the lawless emperors" with this instrument (cf. Fig. 1). By this means, too, he destroyed pagan shrines and restored churches which "the Christ-hating and impious emperors had razed to the ground."[51]

At least in part, communities characterize themselves by those whom they exclude. It would be a distortion to say that the Arabs and Byzantines defined themselves by their relation to each other, as some modern authors treat the concepts of "masculine" and "feminine," and an absurd exaggeration to claim that they therefore constituted one entity not two—one half presupposing the other. But arguments for this polarity, akin to the opposition between civilized Roman and vain, cruel, and greedy barbarian posited by Ammianus Marcellinus, only increased in Byzantium, becoming entwined with the ideological dichotomy between the Orthodox on the one hand and heretics (e.g., Jews and Muslims) on the other.[52] The term heresy (*hairesis*, meaning a sect or school) was used by those who sought to emphasize the rectitude of their own belief. This is the case with Anna Komnene who, in a piece of secular hagiography devoted to her father, the emperor Alexios I, goes on for pages about the "pernicious race of the Bogomils." She does this without recounting the beliefs of these heretics, even while reporting that the emperor's secretary, masquerading as a disciple, wrote down the utterances of their leader, Basil. The omission, she says, is caused by her modesty and by the fact that "though a historian, I am a woman" who did not wish to defile her tongue.[53]

This silence is matched by the absence from the visual record of the end that Basil met, burned at the stake in the polo grounds of the Great Palace. The closest the Byzantines came to such depictions was the indeterminate image of heretics groveling in penance before church councils.[54] If, as I have suggested, the generic was the preferred mode of Orthodox iconography, it must yet be allowed that specificity enters the picture when the Byzantines made works for foreign, and particularly, Latin consumption. This is apparent in a textile depicting the life of St. Lawrence, sent by Michael VIII to his Genoese allies in 1261, that culminates in a scene of Lawrence leading the emperor into his own church in that city.[55] Both in its technique and its depiction of particular events—even if these were imaginary rather than historical—it would seem to be paralleled by a "red samite" altar cloth, recorded in a papal inventory of 1295, that showed the same emperor presented to St. Peter by Pope Gregory X (1271–1296).[56] This pious and political offering was inscribed in both Greek and Latin, a linguistic agglomeration that matched the deliberately hybrid display of its imagery and cult.

Purposeful hybridity is the gesture of one community reaching out to another either in desperation or triumph.[57] Michael VIII's hope for Western aid against the Turks, his readiness to submit to the Roman Church and his gift to the pope testify to the first of these situations. The other extreme is represented by an entire class of objects created in confident absorption of the threat of the alien, not only neutralizing it but turning its accomplishments to the ends of those who made the hybrids. Of this class, recently and enlighteningly studied,[58] perhaps the most telling is a reliquary concocted in late fifteenth-century Germany from a coconut and an Egyptian rock crystal lion together set in a gilded silver mount (Fig. 14). On its face, nothing could seem odder than to make an object of Christian devotion out of the fruit of a strange land and, even more exotically, an animal figurine carved for a Fatimid caliph. The origin of this second component might have meant little to the faithful who came to adore the relic which is today still unidentified and wrapped in a red cloth inside the lion. But in this secondary use the lion ceased to be an Arab carving. Its head was cut off, turned backward to look at the cross, and thus made into an Agnus Dei; the coconut becomes the orb over which the Lamb of God rules. The resultant hybrid is the creation of a culture whose pride it expressed admirably.

In the eyes of post-colonialist historiography, hybridity deforms and weakens established authority;[59] it is the undoer of community, the subversive worm that gets inside the apple and rots it. But in a subtler view the hybrid can revise and invigorate tradition.[60] This opinion rests of course upon one's definition of vigor, a concept that depends upon who is doing the defining. But even the most stern champion of cultural identity would grant that the appropriation and absorption of alien motifs can in many cases be innocuous, neither disturbing nor undermining the essence of communal practice. Thus, for example, the perennial routines of Islamic craftsmanship were left undisturbed when in the thirteenth century metalworkers began to insert motifs borrowed from Christian art into their products. The pairs of haloed figures inlaid in silver in a brass tray now in St. Petersburg wear Western rather than native costumes; their identity is clearly established by the objects that they hold—a censer, a pyxis, a liturgical fan and so on (Fig. 15). While these couples and their accoutrements amount to no specifically Christian program of decoration, Latin or Orthodox, their presence in no way inhibits the function of the object addressed, according to its Arabic inscription, to an anonymous master with the good wishes and blessings customary on Arab metalwork. Rather, the figures are palimpsestically laid over conventions of design and usage long established in the *'ummah*.[61]

Conversely, the Christian world was able, amoeba-like, to ingest alien elements without destroying the organism. If the elements of an icon like the St. George in Athens (Fig. 12) still betray the diversity of their origin, the hybrid nature of the ornament both outside (Fig. 16) and inside the katholikon of the monastery of Hosios Loukas is today perceived only by scholars. Here the pseudo-Kufic lettering enlivens the cut-brick-and-mortar norms of Byzantine architecture. There is no reason to see it as the work of Arab masons. Rather, we can recognize dissonances—signs that were in origin one form of the proclaimed enemy's alphabet—that have become unfamiliar consonances. In this instance, as in others,[62] we are not faced with a "surplus of meanings," that is, the same image interpreted in multiple ways among which none is uniquely authoritative.[63] Here, instead, is an example of adaptation successful because, beyond mere appropriation, the signs were naturalized by virtue of being processed in the minds of the monastery's users and those who worked for them.

Two lessons from the history of modern painting parallel the conclusions to be drawn from this study of the role of art as exponent of Byzantine and Islamic societies. First, if we accept the dictum attributed to Picasso, "I paint objects as I think them, not as I see them," it follows that the cognitive posture of the painter and his public is a determining factor in shaping the artistic production of his time. Second, this shape will change as the painter's posture no longer fits that of those who come after him: Courbet, the great master of French Realism, is said to have remarked "I cannot paint an angel because I have never seen one."[64] It is precisely because angels were part and parcel of the visual experience of Byzantine and medieval Islamic communities that their artists painted them.

Figure 1.   Cross-reliquary, silver gilt and enamel.
Esztergom, Cathedral Treasury

Figure 2.   Chronicle of John Skylitzes. Supplication for the End of a Drought.
Madrid, Biblioteca Nacional, vitr. 26–2, fol. 210v

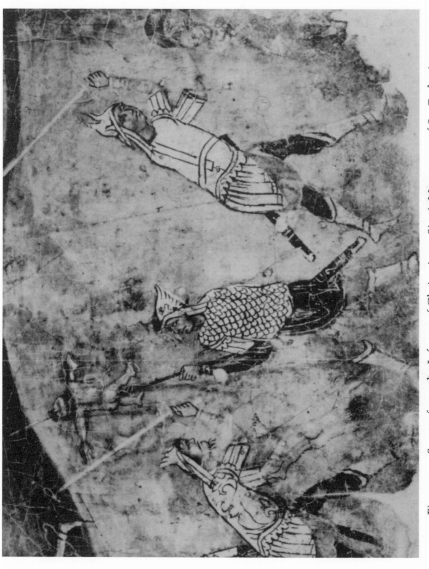

Figure 3.   Scenes from the Infancy of Christ, icon. Sinai. Monastery of St. Catherine

Figure 4.   Baptism of Christ. Mosaic, Nea Moni, Chios

Figure 5.   Paten, agate, silver gilt, enamel, and gemstones.
Paris, Musée du Louvre

Figure 6.   Bishops concelebrating the Liturgy. Apse, Church of
Sts. Peter and Paul, Veliko Turnovo, Bulgaria.
Photograph © 1997, The Metropolitan Museum of Art
(photograph by Bruce White)

Figure 7.   Mosaics in outer octagon, Dome of the Rock, Jerusalem

Figure 8.   Chronicle of John Skylitzes. Triumphal Entry of John I Tzimiskes.
Madrid, Biblioteca Nacional, vitr. 26–2, fol. 172v(a)

Figure 9. Icon of the Mother of God, wool. Sante Fe, N.M.,
Museum of International Folk Art

Figure 10.   Enkolpion-reliquary of St. Demetrios. Back cover, St. George.
© Copyright The British Museum, London

Figure 11.　Enkolpion-reliquary of St. Demetrios. Interior, ciborium of St. Demetrios. © Copyright The British Museum, London

Figure 12.   *Vita* icon of St. George. Athens. Byzantine Museum

Figure 13. St. Symeon Stylites on his column. Menologion of Basil II. Biblioteca Apostolica Vaticana, gr. 1613, fol. 2r

Figure 14. Gothic reliquary, coconut and Fatimid rock crystal.
Münster, Domkammer

Figure 15. Ayyubid tray with Christian figures.
St. Petersburg, Hermitage Museum

Figure 16.   Exterior of the *katholikon* at Hosios Loukas,
with pseudo-Kufic ornament

NOTES

1. *New York Times,* 17 April 1999, p. 1.

2. For the literature, see Alexander Kazhdan and Steven W. Reinert, s.v. Kosovo Polje in *The Oxford Dictionary of Byzantium* (New York, 1991), vol. 2, 1153–54.

3. *The Glory of Byzantium: Art and Culture of the Middle Byzantine Era, A.D. 843–1261,* ed. Helen C. Evans and William D. Wixom (New York, 1997), no. 40 (Jeffrey C. Anderson), where the medallions are not remarked.

4. For this hypothetical mechanism, see Noam Chomsky, *Aspects of the Theory of Syntax* (Cambridge, Mass., 1969).

5. For the part that vision, along with language, plays in the concerns of current cognitive science, see Donald D. Hoffman, *Visual Intelligence: How We Create What We See* (New York, 1999).

6. *The Chronography of Abu'l Faraj,* trans. Ernest A. Wallis Budge (London, 1932) vol. 1, pp. 151, 152, 282.

7. For a selection in silver, silver gilt, and bronze, see *The Glory of Byzantium,* nos. 21–27.

8. *The Chronicle of Joshua the Stylite,* trans. William Wright (Cambridge, 1882), 27.

9. See now Sharon E. J. Gerstel, *Beholding the Sacred Mysteries: Programs of the Byzantine Sanctuary* (Seattle, 1999).

10. Frank E. Brightman, *Liturgies Eastern and Western,* vol. 1 (Oxford, 1896), 377.

11. On such icons at the Church of the Virgin Peribleptos at Ohrid and the Chapel of St. Euthymios at Thessalonike, see Jeffrey C. Anderson in *The Sacred Image East and West,* ed. Robert Ousterhout and Leslie Brubaker (Chicago and Urbana, 1995), 35–36.

12. *Patrologia graeca* 79, col. 577; trans. C. Mango, *Art of the Byzantine Empire, 312–1453* (Englewood Cliffs, N.J., 1972), 32–33.

13. Milton V. Anastos, "The Ethical Theory of Images Formulated by the Iconoclasts in 754 and 815," *Dumbarton Oaks Papers* 8 (1954): 153–60. For the process whereby the individual panel painting assumed an ever more central role in religious practice, see R. Cormack, *Painting the Soul: Icons, Death Masks, and Shrouds* (London, 1997).

14. Anthony Cutler, "Art in Byzantine Society: Motive Forces of Byzantine Patronage," *Jahrbuch der österreichischen Byzantinistik* 31, no. 2 (1982): 760–62.

15. Nikos Zias, "Panagia Protothrone at Chalke" in *Naxos,* ed. Manolis Chatzidakis (Athens, 1989), 30.

16. *Church History,* 6.10, trans. Robert Payne Smith (Oxford, 1860), 401.

17. Sharon E.J. Gerstel, "Ritual Swimming and the Feast of Epiphany," *Abstracts of the Byzantine Studies Conference* 21 (1995): 78.

18. Early accessible examples in a variety of media are illustrated in Richard Ettinghausen and Oleg Grabar, *The Art and Architecture of Islam, 650–1250* (New Haven and London, 1987), figs. 189, 192, 194, 196, 197, 201. For a more considered statement—and one that does not fall into the opposite error of viewing such scenes as foretastes of a Muslim heaven—see Ettinghausen, "Early Realism in Islamic Art," in *Studi orientalistici in onore di Giorgio Levi della Vida* (Rome, 1956), vol. 1, 250–73.

19. Ed. Ghada al-Hijjawi al-Qaddumi (Cambridge, Mass., 1996). An instance of the transcultural appeal of the embellished paten is perhaps afforded by Pachymeres' story of a copper *plateia* found beautiful enough to be laden with autumn fruits and offered to the emperor Michael VIII. Before its presentation, however, it was discovered that the dish's "Egyptian" inscription contained the name of Mohammed, a discovery that utterly disqualified it. See George Pachymeres, *Relations historiques* 6.12, ed. Albert Failler (Paris, 1984), 573–75.

20. *The Glory of Byzantium*, no. 28 (Helen C. Evans).

21. Christopher Walter and Gordana Babić, "The Inscriptions upon Liturgical Rolls in Byzantine Apse Decoration," *Revue des études byzantines* 34 (1976): 243–80.

22. Thus one inscription on the outer face of the octagon reads "Praise be to God who begets no son and who has no associate and who has no surrogate. . . ."

23. I borrow the phrase from Oleg Grabar, *The Shape of the Holy: Early Islamic Jerusalem* (Princeton, N.J., 1996). See esp. pp. 56–75 for an insightful examination of this body of decoration. To this should be added the account of a vision related by al-Tabari (*Annales*, ed. Michael Jan de Goeje [Leiden, 1879–1880] III, I, pp. 534–35) concerning al-Ma'mūn's grandfather al-Mahdī (775–785), who ordered al-Walīd's name in an inscription in the Mosque of the Prophet at Medīna to be replaced with his own. Like the story of the emperor's vision of St. Irene of Chrysobalanton (note 26 below), it suggests the major role of apparitions in the visual communities with which we are concerned. As to acts of appropriation, it is interesting to note the report that the ruins of Babylon are now being rebuilt with bricks that bear the name of Saddam Hussein. See the *New York Times*, 9 May 1999, p. 7.

24. Irene Bierman, *Writing Signs: The Fatimid Public Text* (Berkeley and Los Angeles, 1998), 53–54.

25. Cf. the inscription around the apse mosaic of Hagia Sophia, Constantinople, set up in 867: "The images which the impostors had cast down here pious emperors have again set up." Only a small portion of the

text survives *in situ;* it is known completely from the *Greek Anthology.*
See also note 51, below.

26. *Acta Sanctorum,* Julii 6, 628E–629A.

27. Paul Lemerle, *Les plus anciens receuils des Miracles de Saint-Démétrius et la pénétration des Slaves dans les Balkans,* vol. 1 (Paris, 1978), p. 115, lines 16–17; p. 162, lines 16–17; cf. p. 102, line 9.

28. Ibid., 1, p. 135, lines 8–9; p. 157, lines 15–20.

29. On the Emperor Maurice's desire for such an auxiliary, see Paul Lemerle, "Notes sur les plus anciens représentations de Saint-Démétrius," *Deltion tes Christianikes Archaiologikes Hetaireias* 10 (1980–1981): 7.

30. Of Christ and St. Peter and, in another version of the *Life,* these together with the Mother of God. See Cynthia J. Stallman, *The Life of St. Pancratius of Taormina,* doctoral dissertation, Oxford University, 1986, 2 vols.

31. Vitalien Laurent, "Une homélie inédite de l'archévêque de Thessalonique Léon le Philosophie sur l'Annonciation," in *Mélanges Eugène Tisserant,* Studi e testi 232 (Rome, 1964), 2, p. 301, lines 146–49.

32. *The Travels of Ibn Jubayr,* trans. Ronald J.C. Broadhurst (London, 1952), 295–96.

33. Gerstel, *Beholding the Sacred Mysteries,* 12.

34. But see Sophia Kalopissi-Verti, *Dedicatory Inscriptions and Donor Portraits in Thirteenth-Century Churches of Greece* (Vienna, 1992).

35. Thus Saladin ordered the name of the Fatimid caliph al-Ādid to be dropped from the *khutba* when the latter died in 1171. See al-Maqrizi, *A History of Ayyubid Sultans of Egypt,* trans. Ronald J.C. Broadhurst (Boston, 1980), 37. (The structural relation of such mentions to the readings of names from the diptychs in Christian liturgies is self-evident). Verbal citation and its complement, erasure, had long been practiced in Islam as witnessed by the inclusion of the names of the ruler and other figures of high rank on the *tiraz* bands embroidered on garments produced in state workshops. In the early ninth century, for example, the caliph al-Ma'mūn ordered the removal of the name of his brother, whom he suspected of plotting his deposition, to be struck from the *tiraz.* See the *History of al-Tabarī,* vol. 31, trans. Michael Fishbein (Albany, N.Y., 1992), 23.

36. F. Miklosich and J. Müller, *Acta et diplomata graeca medii aevi sacra et profana,* vol. 1 (Vienna, 1860), 221–26.

37. Trans. Angeliki Laiou in *Holy Women of Byzantium,* ed. Alice-Mary Talbot (Washington, D.C., 1996), 260.

38. For icons in such a setting see Anthony Cutler, *The Hand of the Master: Craftsmanship, Ivory and Society in Byzantium (9th–11th Centuries)* (Princeton, N.J., 1994), 237.

39. *Michael Italikos, Lettres et discours,* ed. Paul Gautier (Paris, 1972), 209–210.

40. *Das Eparchenbuch Leons des Weisen*, vol. 1, bk. 3, ed. Johannes Koder (Vienna, 1991), 74–76.

41. I borrow the translations from the catalogue entry by Dimitrios Katsarelis in *The Glory of Byzantium*, no. 116. Here, too, the original Greek and an account of the object's history.

42. A rough analogy in the Muslim world would be the shrine containing the head of al-Husayn ibn 'Ali, the grandson of the Prophet. Ibn al-Zubayr describes it in Cairo where it is said to be kept "in a silver casket and over it has been built a mausoleum so superb as to be beyond description and the powers of the mind to comprehend." See *The Travels of Ibn Jubayr* (as in note 32 above), 36–37. The relic is said to have been displayed earlier in the Umayyad Mosque in Damascus (ibid., 280).

43. See *The Glory of Byzantium*, no. 117 (Ioli Kalavrezou), where the object is for an unexplained reason assigned to a date perhaps as much as a century later than the similar *enkolpion* in London.

44. Hans Belting, "Introduction" in *Il Medio Oriente e l'Occidente nell'arte del XIII secolo*, Atti del XXIV Congresso Internazionale di Storia dell'arte, vol. 2 (Bologna, 1982), 3.

45. Manolis Chatzidakis in Kurt Weitzmann, M. Chatzidakis, Krsto Miatev, and Svetozar Radojčič, *Frühe Ikonen* (Vienna and Munich, 1965), p. xxvi and fig. 49.

46. Anthony Cutler, *The Aristocratic Psalters in Byzantium* (Paris, 1984), 64–65 and fig. 248.

47. Lemerle, *Les plus anciens recueils*, vol. 1, 177–78.

48. See note 19 above.

49. *Digenis Akritis: The Grottaferrata and Escorial Versions*, ed. and trans. Elizabeth Jeffreys (Cambridge, 1998), pp. 120–21, lines 907, 911; pp. 194–95, lines 736–39.

50. Nicephorus, Patriarch of Constantinople, *Short History* (Washington, D.C., 1990), p. 66, lines 12–14.

51. Cited in Philostorgius, *Kirchengeschichte*, ed. Joseph Bidez and Friedhelm Winkelmann (Berlin, 1972), Anhang I, 154–55. Although John is otherwise unknown, this portion of his text is evidently one model for the apse inscription in Hagia Sophia, cited above.

52. On the visual expression of these equations, see Kathleen Corrigan, *Visual Polemics in the Ninth-Century Byzantine Psalters* (Cambridge, 1992).

53. *The Alexiad of the Princess Anna Comnena*, trans. Elizabeth A. S. Dawes (London, 1928), 415–19. The Bogomils held the material world to be the creation and realm of the devil and denied most of the basic doctrines of the Orthodox Church, including the Incarnation.

54. E.g., the submission of Makedonios before the First Council of Constantinople in the ninth-century MS, Paris, B.N. gr. 510 (Henri Omont,

Miniatures des plus anciens manuscrit grecs de la Bibliothèque Nationale [Paris, 1929], pl. 50). It is possible that scenes such as the fate of Basil the Bogomil shaped depictions of the fires of the Last Judgment. This was proposed by Nancy P. Ševčenko at a symposium at Dumbarton Oaks in May 1999.

55. Belting in *Il Medio Oriente e l'Occidente*, p. 2 and fig. 1.

56. Émile Molinier in *Bibliothèque de l'Ecole des Chartes* 46 (1885): 18–19, no. 811.

57. For a theoretical scrutiny of the context in which such gestures originate, see Robert J.C. Young, *Colonial Desire: Hybridity in Theory, Culture and Race* (London, 1995). I am grateful to Claire Farago for drawing my attention to this work.

58. See Avinoam Shalem, *Islam Christianized: Islamic Portable Objects in the Medieval Church Treasures of the West* (Frankfurt am Main, 1996).

59. Homi K. Bhahba, "Signs Taken for Wonders: Questions of Ambivalence and Authority Under a Tree outside Delhi, May 1817," *Critical Inquiry* 12 (1985): 114–65.

60. Claire Farago, "Introduction" in *Reframing the Renaissance: Visual Culture in Europe and Latin America* (London and New Haven, 1995), 12.

61. I borrow the useful notion of the palimpsest from Young, *Colonial Desire*, 24, 173, and passim.

62. A. Cutler, "The 'Mythological' Bowl in the Treasury of San Marco at Venice," in *Near Eastern Numismatics, Iconography, Epigraphy, and History: Studies in Honor of George C. Miles*, ed. Dikran K. Kouymjian (Beirut, 1974), 235–54.

63. Farago, "Introduction," 12.

64. I have been unable to verify the origin of this statement or that of Picasso cited above. Both are widespread in the popular literature on these painters. The lack of demonstrable authenticity of course does not limit their utility as embodiments of mental attitudes.

CHAPTER THREE

"Illustris patriarcha Joseph": Jean Gerson, Representations of Saint Joseph, and Imagining Community among Churchmen in the Fifteenth Century

Pamela Sheingorn

"Rally Taps Men's Desire for Sense of Community" asserts a headline in the *New York Times* for Sunday, October 5, 1997. The rhetoric of the group that organized the rally, the Promise Keepers, develops causal connections between its concept of community—that "men of God" should stand together—and morality, both in the nation and in the family. According to the Promise Keepers, the restoration of morality depends upon men enacting responsibly their roles as husbands and fathers, as heads of families. Though the Promise Keepers are unlikely to have been aware of it, the idea linking male authority in the Christian family with the restoration of morality in the society at large had been enunciated in the fifteenth century by Jean Gerson, who chose Joseph, husband of the Virgin Mary, as the symbol of his cause. Further, Gerson presented his program to men of God, the churchmen gathered at the Council of Constance in 1416, who represented for him the "imagined community" of Christendom.

Jean Gerson, Chancellor of the University of Paris in the first two decades of the fifteenth century,[1] worried about whether women were keeping to their place. As female literacy rose rapidly, Gerson worried that women's ability to read and write love letters might lead them to sin.[2] He worried about what he saw as women's pretense to learning: "They wish to speak and dispute about theology more than many a great theologian, and wishing to judge sermons and reprove preachers, they say of one that he has told a story from the Bible badly, and of another that he is teaching heresy; and when they have an opinion fixed in their heads, nothing will get rid of it."[3] Gerson worried about "deluded visionaries," especially when they communicated to others what they had learned in their visions; he even had doubts about the revelations of Bridget of Sweden.[4] Generally suspect of women as teachers and inclined to harp on the apostolic prohibition against women preaching, Gerson was incensed when women presumed to teach men more learned than themselves, when they had the temerity "to call priests of God their sons, and to teach them the profession in which they have been carefully trained."[5]

Gerson also monitored representations of women. Though a devotee of the Virgin Mary, Gerson did not approve of a new kind of Marian image in sculpture called the "vierge ouvrante"—the virgin that opens. These statues, usually made of wood or ivory, portrayed Mary standing, often holding the child Jesus in her arms. The statue's body could be opened, rather like a winged altarpiece, and when opened revealed an interior space that functioned as a sacrament shrine and housed a representation of the Trinity.[6] Gerson "saw nothing of beauty or devotion" in such statues, and feared that they would lead "simple people" to the mistaken conclusion that "the entire Trinity had taken human flesh inside the Virgin Mary."[7] Gerson understood the power of images,[8] especially those that gave human form to the divine and created relationships between God and humans, and his queasiness about the "vierge ouvrante" reveals both the proliferation of such representations in the fifteenth century and a conservative reaction to them. Based at least in part in what has been called the feminization of religion in the late Middle Ages, Gerson's worries about the roles and representations of women in late medieval religion exemplify what R. N. Swanson calls a "real issue" at that time:

"the possible marginalization of the male, and more particularly of the masculine."[9]

But this anxiety about gender was not the only trouble spot in fifteenth-century religion. The Great Schism had begun in 1379, and, so long as there was more than one pope, the unity of the Church was fractured. Called "the most influential theologian of his day," Jean Gerson worked assiduously to end the Schism and restore the Church to its former unity.[10] As chancellor of the University of Paris, he might realistically have expected to have a significant impact on the Schism, the beginning of which he blamed on a woman, Catherine of Siena.[11] Though he worked toward the goal of healing the Schism in many different ways, Gerson selected a particular symbol under whose aegis the healing might be effected: Joseph the carpenter, husband of the Virgin Mary. As Rosemary Hale notes, "Josephine imagery is the chief building block for his attempts to mend the ecclesiastical fractures of the Great Schism; the Church, in need of protection and unity, should champion the symbolism inherent in the character of Joseph."[12] Gerson's efforts contributed materially to the healing of the Schism, but, ironically, the council that ended the Schism declined to adopt Joseph as the patron saint of the universal Church; one of the reasons, I argue in this essay, was that Gerson chose badly; he could not control the cultural meanings attached to Joseph, meanings that precluded Joseph's effective shaping into a symbol around which a community of Christian men would rally.

At first glance, Gerson's choice seems ideal: Joseph the carpenter, husband of the Virgin Mary and step-father of Jesus, had a very restricted cult before the fifteenth century, but had begun to receive some recognition. In 1399 a feast in honor of Joseph was made obligatory for members of the Franciscan order.[13] Further, Joseph was indisputably biblical; the New Testament opens with his genealogy (Matthew 1:1–17), attesting to his descent from the house of David. Joseph's close association with the early life of Jesus could not be questioned. Joseph must therefore have appeared to be available for shaping to Gerson's purposes. In order to gain some insight into Gerson's choice of Joseph we need to begin with a concept fundamental to his world view, the concept of order, which to Gerson meant hierarchy.

For Gerson, hierarchical order characterizes the heavens; the created universe reflects that order, which is especially evident in the Church.[14] As Louis B. Pascoe writes, "Just as the angelic orders are subordinated to one head which is God, so too are patriarchs, archbishops, bishops, archpriests, and priests subordinated to the one visible head of the church, the pope. The church, then, in imitation of the angelic kingdom, is hierarchically ordered in all its members under the one head."[15] Gerson felt this hierarchy to be indispensable; without it, such chaos would result that *Christianitas* itself would be endangered.[16]

Hierarchy was fundamental to Gerson's understanding of human relationships as well. In a sermon he preached in 1408, in the presence of the king of France, Gerson described how human society would have functioned before the Fall of Adam and Eve; though laws, coercive justice, and political rule would all have been unnecessary, there would still have been a need for the rule of "father over son, of man over woman, of the more wise over the less wise, of reason over the non-rational."[17] For Gerson, the hierarchy of the sexes also forms not only the most basic, but in fact an indispensable principle of marriage; he writes: "Between two men or two women there cannot be a sacrament of marriage . . . for in a marriage there must be in one of the parties a perfect and active virtue (*vertus*), which is in the man, and he represents God; and in the other party there must be weakness and passive virtue, which is in the woman, and she represents holy church and the soul."[18]

To theorize Gerson's views we might invoke closure theory as set out by Frank Parkin.[19] For Gerson, order resulted from "exclusionary closure," a "downward exercise of power" by means of which one group attempts to keep another in a subordinate position; its mode is "collectivist," that is, birth into the group is all that is needed for access to its privileges. So, for example, being born as a male meant that one had in oneself "perfect and active virtue," whereas birth as a female guaranteed "weakness and passive virtue." But the subordinated group may respond by attempting "usurpationary closure," or "the use of power in an upward direction." The "feminization of religion" must have appeared to Gerson to be such an attempted usurpation.

Perhaps one reason that Gerson clung so firmly to his principle of hierarchy was that the institution within which he functioned was not in order, not only with regard to gender, but in other ways as well. As Pascoe summarizes the situation,

> Fragmented by the Great Schism which had lasted since 1378, plagued by numerous heresies, especially those of Wyclif and Hus, submerged under extensive moral corruption, the church of Gerson's times was hardly a true image of its celestial archetype. Innumerable deformities in its hierarchical structure had occurred, notably the deformity introduced by the lack of a single head. . . . The calamities that befell the church were always regarded by Gerson essentially as perversions of the duly constituted hierarchical order.[20]

The worst of these, however, was the Schism, "the greatest deformity in the church's order since it affected all Christians whether good or bad."[21]

With Joseph, Gerson saw a way to restore order to the Christian community, from the microcosm of the family to the macrocosm of the Church. Gerson says that he learned to champion Joseph from his mentor, Pierre d'Ailly,[22] and he agitated for a feast day in honor of Joseph, who had no recognition in the Roman calendar. In 1413 Gerson wrote a letter to the universal Church promoting this cause and offering to make available for a new liturgy of Joseph some texts that he had himself composed.[23] Gerson preached sermons, wrote tracts, and twisted arms on behalf of his saint, but his most significant effort came at a general council convened to end the Schism and reform the Church, the Council of Constance. Gerson attended this council, "destined to be the largest of its kind," as delegate for the king of France, the University of Paris, and the ecclesiastical province of Sens.[24] At its start he was, in John Morrall's words, "after [emperor] Sigismund, the man of the hour."[25]

On September 8, 1416, for the feast of the Nativity of the Virgin, Gerson preached a sermon to the Council of Constance, taking as his text Matthew 1:16: "And Jacob begot Joseph the husband of Mary, of whom was born Jesus, who is called Christ."[26] One of the most popular preachers of his day, Gerson brought all his ingenuity to bear upon this text, extrapolating from it qualities of Joseph that justify his elevation to sainthood. Gerson says he will use a procedure of moving from naturally known principles to conclusions drawn either from evidence or from probable consequences. Thus from his biblical text he takes two principles: 1) Mary was mother of God and 2) Joseph was the husband of Mary and thus her head, because the man is the head of the woman according to the Apostle (that is, Paul). It follows from these two principles that whatever praises belong to Mary belong also to Joseph, since he was selected by God to be her fitting spouse. Gerson argues four main points: that Mary and Joseph were noble, sanctified in the womb,[27] free of concupiscence, and parents of Jesus according to the concept of the manifold nativity. The text of this sermon, which represents the culmination of his campaign for Joseph, reveals that Gerson's revision of Joseph was an attempt to bring him into conformity with Gerson's ideal of masculinity, an ideal appropriate to a celibate cleric.

Joseph's nobility derives not so much from his double descent from the royal house of David as from his "servitude in bodily compliance to God" which, being superior to any other person's service to God, paradoxically rendered Joseph most noble.[28] Nonetheless, Gerson argued elsewhere, "the royals and high nobility ought to have special devotion as much for saint Joseph as for Our Lady because of their royal and worthy nobility."[29] Sanctification in the womb contributed to Joseph's total lack of concupiscence. This allowed Gerson to argue that Joseph was not an old man, as apocryphal texts had wrongly insisted and as painters had represented him.[30] Rather, Gerson asserts, Joseph was about thirty-six when he married the Virgin; the strength of physical maturity was crucial for Joseph's assigned task of protecting Mary.

Gerson tries out a number of arguments that, though virginal, Joseph was nonetheless father to Jesus. He suggests that "because the body of Mary belonged to Joseph by matrimonial law, by which it comes about by mutual transfer that the body of the man belongs to the woman and vice versa, let us see if with intelligent sobriety it is permissible to us to say that Christ Jesus was born from the body and flesh of Joseph." He is, however, concerned that this reasoning might be "a stumbling-block to pious ears," and settles for more conventional arguments.[31]

But it often seems most important to Gerson that Joseph was the head of the household, a role recognized by both Mary and Jesus. He addresses Joseph directly: "O incomparable dignity that the mother of God, queen of heaven, lady of the world, did not consider it unworthy to call you lord." Mary's essential quality of "humility" complements Joseph's "sublimity" and "incomparable dignity."[32] As he had explained in his "Considérations sur saint Joseph," "And it is not at all to be doubted that her humility was so great that she rendered herself as much, or more, subject to her loyal spouse Joseph as any other woman should and is able to be to her spouse."[33] Gerson speaks of a "chain of natural obligation" according to which Mary and Jesus recognize the "authority, principality, domination, and imperium" belonging to Joseph as husband and father.[34] We might say that Gerson works very hard in this sermon to associate Joseph with the "exclusionary closure" enjoyed by men. He constitutes an earthly trinity of Joseph, Mary, and Jesus, which is to be admired and venerated.

Though he unequivocally condemns the apocryphal texts that for him are filled with lies about Joseph, Gerson also ventures beyond the Gospels to create a number of plausible though nonbiblical scenes, among them Joseph's death in the presence of Mary and Jesus.[35] "It is fitting to believe that Jesus wept for his dying father and the blessed virgin for her dying spouse. . . . 'My husband,' she cries out, 'are you going? You abandon and leave behind a suffering widow . . . farewell, beloved.'"[36] Again Gerson emphasizes Mary's dependence on Joseph.

Having unfolded all his reasons that Joseph should receive his own feast day, Gerson ends with a direct appeal to his audience, telling them that if they have agreed with his conclusions about Joseph, they will institute a feast in Joseph's honor, either for the virginal marriage of Mary and Joseph or for his "blessed departure." "And why? So that through the merits and the intercession of a patron so great, so mighty, and powerful with regard to his spouse, who bore Jesus called Christ, the Church will be returned to her one true and certain husband, the Pope, her spouse, the vicar of Christ." In sum, the Church should submit to the rule of Joseph.[37]

In this sermon, Gerson works carefully with hierarchical pairs: Mary submits to Joseph as the Church submits to Christ. In order to be in that relationship, the Church must have a pope, and the figure under whose aegis the Church can resolve its crisis and return to a single pope must be Joseph. The metaphor of Christ and the Church as *sponsus* and *sponsa* derives, of course, from exegesis of the Song of Songs, and was well known to Gerson through his familiarity with Bernard of Clairvaux's sermons on the Song of Songs.[38] Reading the *sponsa* as Mary rather than the Church, which produces the hierarchical pair Christ-Mary, was usual in Gerson's time.[39] Also to be found in earlier exegesis is the substitution of Joseph for Christ, perhaps most explicitly stated by Peter Olivi: "Joseph represents the Father-God, or Christ, for he is the *sponsus* of the Church."[40] But Gerson brings these relationships to bear on a contemporary ecclesiastical and social problem by slipping from one gendered pairing to another—not only from Christ-Church, to Pope (vicar of Christ)–Church, but also from Christ-Mary to Joseph-Mary. This last pair is justified not only by Mary's humility but also by the hierarchy of male over female, which, as we have seen, Gerson viewed as natural. The hierarchy of gender runs in the same direction in all of these pairings. Thus the weakness in the Church—the Schism—becomes a weakness in patriarchy, and the installation of Joseph would repair the weakness. Judith Bennett defines patriarchy as "a complex system of male dominance rooted in ideology, culture, and society, . . . a system that has . . . adapted remarkably well to the conflicts, contradictions, and confusions it produces."[41] Gerson's proposition to honor Joseph can be understood as his attempt to mend the patriarchal system, to counter the increasing "feminization of religion" that he saw around him. His goal was the restoration of order, from the microcosm to the macrocosm—from the husband-wife unit to the Church itself.

Given the prestige of Paris-trained theologians, Gerson had every right to expect that the Council of Constance would applaud his choice of Joseph as the symbol of its efforts to restore unity to the Church. The Council had repeatedly consulted him and other Paris doctors and masters and had followed their advice.[42] But Joseph was not assigned a feast day by the Council of Constance. Why did Gerson fail? Certainly one immediate reason may lie in the precise historical circumstances of the Council, for by the time Gerson preached his sermon tensions had arisen between the French representatives on the one hand and the English and German representatives on the other. But I want to argue here that there were other reasons as well, based in the representations of Joseph in circulation and on Gerson's gender hierarchy.

Although he knew of the negative aspects of Joseph's representation in late medieval culture, Gerson seems to have badly underestimated their tenacity. A survey of the representations of Joseph in circulation in the late fourteenth and early fifteenth centuries reveals the many ways that the late medieval Joseph was ill suited for the role Gerson envisioned.

A Franciscan emphasis on Joseph's poverty and humility can be traced at least as far back as Bonaventure, who, in a sermon for the vigil of the Nativity, posed the rhetorical question, "Why was Mary united in marriage with the little peasant (*rusticello*) Joseph?"[43] Elsewhere he gave three reasons that Joseph had been chosen as Mary's spouse: his lineage, his fidelity, and "on account of poverty; because Christ above all came to confound pride he did not wish to be called the son of a king but the son of a workman."[44] As a man who "lived by the work of his own hands" (vicit de labore manuum suarum),[45] Joseph was suited to the humble circumstances of the Nativity so important to Saint Francis and to Franciscan spirituality. For Bonaventure, it was precisely Joseph's humility, his reverence for Jesus and Mary, that made him a model for others.[46] One of the most widely circulating Franciscan texts, the *Meditaciones vite Christi* now attributed to Johannes de Caulibus, takes humility and poverty as its twin themes. Reporting on the life of Jesus from his twelfth to his thirtieth year, the author writes, "And consider above all other things that blessed family, small but very, very excellent, leading a poor and humble life. Happy old Joseph sought what he could [earn] from his skill as a woodworker."[47] Illustrations to the *Meditaciones*, which was translated into several vernaculars, portray Joseph as a humble workman.[48]

Joseph's representations frequently include signs that identify him as a peasant. For example, in the Anglo-Norman *Holkham Bible* Joseph cultivates the earth with his iron-shod spade.[49] Part and parcel of his peasant identity was Joseph's suspicion of Mary, his assumption that he had been made a cuckold by his young wife.[50] Closely related to the fabliau tradition and favorite subject of medieval drama,[51] the narrative of Joseph's doubt held up to ridicule the dull-witted clod who could not grasp God's plan, even as it articulated the doubts many audience members must also have felt about Mary's pregnancy. Thought of as fond of his drink, Joseph was sometimes represented as what Ruth Mellinkoff calls a "guzzler," another display of gross behavior associating him with the peasantry.[52]

Old age characterized Joseph in the fourteenth and early fifteenth centuries. In representations he usually grasps a crutch-staff as emblem of his old age, but frequently his body is visibly old as well. Two stories from the acts of Dorothy of Montau (d. 1394), who had an elderly husband named Adalbert, illustrate how completely Joseph was identified with old age; in the first a priest marvels that so pretty, devout, and courteous a woman as Dorothy "should sustain reproaches and blows so patiently from that old Joseph!"[53] In the other, when Dorothy and her husband were on pilgrimage, someone they encountered jokingly asked Dorothy "if she were carrying Joseph to the fountain of youth."[54] As these anecdotes reveal, the situation of a young woman married to an old man tended to be viewed negatively and to be treated as a subject for satirical and ridiculing humor.[55]

The immense popularity of Mary also led to representations that gave her authority over Joseph. In the *Queen Mary Psalter*, for example, the scene of Jesus in the Temple features what Ann Rudloff Stanton has characterized as a "shrunken Joseph," a diminutive and wizened figure who clearly defers to the Virgin towering over him. For Gerson such an inversion of the "natural" hierarchy of the sexes, a move toward "usurpationary closure," would have exemplified the need for reform.[56]

Joseph also remains in the margins of sacred history. Since the biblical text does not mention him as present during the Adoration of the Magi, he often hovers in the background or sits on the ground in representations of that scene. Frequently his placement in scenes of the Nativity associates him with the animals in the stable (which might also reinforce his identity as peasant). In other Nativity scenes he tends a cooking pot over a fire, presumably making porridge for the infant Jesus;[57] Joseph's attempt to feed the infant becomes a scene of raucous humor in a German Nativity play.[58] This attention to the material takes a less pleasant turn when Joseph is portrayed as a miser, claiming the Magi's offerings in order to store them in a treasure chest.[59] Although this quality may be an indirect reference to a negative stereotype of Jews as greedy and grasping, many other images explicitly identify Joseph as a Jew by giving him a distinctively shaped hat.[60]

In Nativity scenes, Joseph's most characteristic gesture of head resting in hand may also mark him as a Jew, especially after the twelfth century. Understood as a visual sign of meditative melancholy or mourning, the gesture is generally taken by art historians to refer either to Joseph's sorrow that the Incarnation will be rejected by his people, the Jews, or to his melancholic doubt about Mary's virginity. Heublein argues that the reference is sometimes to Joseph's meditation upon the future sacrificial death of the infant, but when combined with the Jew's hat, beard, and staff turns Joseph into a "personification of 'ignorant Judaism.'"[61] The reception of the gesture may well have shifted after humoral medicine spread in the West in the twelfth century, because intellectuals employed the theory of the humors to label Jews as melancholic: sad, pallid, and antisocial.[62] A later commentary on the *De secretis mulierum* discussing hemorrhoids and melancholic men notes, "This [hemorrhoidal bleeding] is found in Jews more than in others, for their natures are more melancholic."[63] We may conclude that the association of Jews with melancholy persisted into Gerson's time. The gesture of head resting in hand and its affect must have been readily associated with Joseph in popular culture, since in a sermon delivered in Florence in 1424 Bernardino of Siena decries the "foolish artists [who] paint him as a sad old man with his hand on his cheek as if he were in pain or depressed."[64] Bernardino's vivid description of contemporary representations of Joseph indicates clearly the image in the popular imagination that Gerson was attempting to redraw.

Finally, art contemporary with Gerson had a tendency to marginalize Joseph by visualizing God the Father, Mary the mother, and Jesus as a self-contained unit; this unit may be read as the Oedipal triangle of Symbolic Father, Symbolic Mother, and ego (child). I have written elsewhere about the embodiment of the Father God in late medieval art, and his claims to masculinity and paternity, that is, to the Name-of-the-Father, which underlie some of my argument in this essay.[65] Representations of the Nativity from the early fifteenth century give literal visualization to the Oedipal triangle by placing God the Father in the sky above the manger while the Virgin and the Child occupy the corners of an isosceles triangle with God at its apex (Fig. 1). In some examples words assigned to God the Father issue from his mouth and form the side of the triangle the corner of which is the Child; they make the unequivocal claim, "Hic est filius meus"—this is my son. Joseph, who is relegated to a secondary position outside the triangle, is excluded both visually and verbally.

Jean Gerson was thus attempting to reconstruct a figure bur-
dened by characteristics that rendered him abject: "a notion desig-
nating his degraded or cast out status within the terms of sociality,"
as Judith Butler puts it.[66] Abjection further "presupposes and produces a domain of agency from which it is differentiated."[67] The
agency of God the Father functions to degrade Joseph and to
reduce his role to virtual meaninglessness.

Further, late medieval representations of Joseph dissociate
him from the kind of dominant masculinity Gerson needed to
create for him. Almost every one of the traits associated with Joseph in the period up to 1420 participates in assigning Joseph a
subordinate masculinity. The Franciscan quality of humility is
one that Gerson himself assigns to women, not men. Referring to
the visual culture of this period, Hans Nieuwdorp refers to Joseph's
"submissive, nurturing and unmanly role."[68] To the extent that he
was identified with Judaism, Joseph may have been feminized, as
Steven Kruger has argued in his study of "The Bodies of Jews in
the Late Middle Ages."[69] His identification as a peasant also dis-
tanced Joseph from dominant masculinity, especially from the
cultural type of the knight. According to Paul Freedman:

> peasants were often depicted as filthy, subhuman, and comical,
> the reverse of the civilized and courtly. In medieval literature,
> the *vilain* was everything that the knight was not: lowly,
> servile, gross, materialistic, cowardly, malformed, and unfit for
> the service of love. Above all, the rustic, more specifically the
> *male* rustic, represented gross materiality. Peasants appeared in
> art and iconography as coarse and ill-favored. Likened to domes-
> tic animals or (by means of images of filth and excrement) to
> the land he tilled, the peasant was rendered as large, grotesque,
> and rather sluggish. He craved food, yawned, scratched himself,
> was partial to drink, and enjoyed sleeping.[70]

Joseph's enfeebled age, but even more his visible exclusion from
any claim to paternity, also threatened his masculinity. Vern Bullough suggests that by the end of the Middle Ages "masculinity is
identified with potency and any sign of lack of virility is a threat
to one's definition as a man."[71]

Gerson was redesigning Joseph to do a man's job, but the Joseph
familiar to his audiences did not sufficiently correlate with the

dominant masculinities in circulation, whether of young men or old. The youthful man was viewed as a sexual predator, employing the techniques recommended for seducing women in the widely read *Romance of the Rose.* The *Rose* was so popular that Gerson preached against it, and Christine de Pisan denounced its vision of masculinity as predatory. Gerson tried to move the notion of Joseph's age to that of maturity, the third of the four ages of man, so that he would have the physical wherewithall to offer effective physical protection to Mary and her child. However, an illustration of the four ages from a French translation of the most popular encyclopedia in circulation at the time, Bartholomeus Anglicus's *On the Nature of Things,* shows the mature man in armor; the chivalric male protected women and children by fighting. He assured his masculinity by using his prowess to gain honor and by remaining staunchly faithful to his lord.[72] This mature male also had firm control of his family; an illustration from a French manuscript containing Aristotle's *Politics, Economics,* and *Ethics* shows how such a man maintains an emotional distance from his family even as he shapes wife and children to his will.[73] The timid and doubtful old Joseph of Gerson's day could not be so quickly altered to fit the role Gerson assigned him of asserting his authority to return both women and the Church to submissive roles.

Slow changes in the gender characteristics of Joseph occur in the course of the fifteenth century, and these changes must have been due in no small part to the wide circulation of Gerson's writings. As D. Catherine Brown notes, "Even before the end of the fifteenth century there had been six printed editions of his complete works apart from the numerous manuscripts and printed editions of single works or selected groups of his writings that were produced during the century."[74] Through his texts about Joseph, Gerson provided a way to employ the visual in the gender struggle. R. N. Swanson suggests how this might have happened:

Possibly, then, men in the later middle ages — and perhaps earlier — resented the female aspect of religion, which was arguably derived from its Incarnational emphases, and sought to recreate a Christianity more to their liking. If this is so, then the problem of religion as a battleground between the genders may have been increasingly intense in the fifteenth century. As men claimed a greater stake in religion, and one which was

almost necessarily patriarchal if women's place was to be
wrested from them, so the tensions increased.[75]

If we adopt Swanson's metaphor, then we might view the construction of Joseph as one of the fronts on that battlefield. But so
far as that front was concerned, the battle was not easily won.
Though new gender characteristics are wielded in the attempt to
overwrite the characteristics we have just surveyed, those characteristics display noteworthy tenacity. A survey of representations
from 1420 to the early sixteenth century will illustrate this point.

Increasingly, bodily signs allow the viewer to place Joseph's
age at around forty, in conformity with Gerson's Joseph: his back
is straight, not bent, and his hair and beard are brown, or only
touched with grey. We see this more youthful Joseph in the Nativity from the Flemish *Hastings Hours,* made before 1483 (Fig. 2),
where he nonetheless retains his peasant hood. Further, his lack of
a halo and the pale color of his garment that allows him to fade
into the background definitely do not wrest primacy of place from
Mary, who occupies the foreground center, has a golden halo, and
wears an eye-catching highly saturated blue robe.[76] And even
youth is not assured to Joseph in the fifteenth century; the drama
appears to retain the old Joseph, as in the *Passion of Semur,* which
was copied in 1485. When he introduces himself and before he is
selected to be Mary's husband, Joseph emphasizes one quality—
his advanced age: "Ah, good people, I'm old. / The virgin would be
quite destroyed/to have such a greybeard."[77]

In a wood sculpture from Alsace dated about 1500 (Fig. 3),
Joseph's brown beard may signify his youthful age, but the child
who tugs at it deprives Joseph of any shred of patriarchal authority.
It has been argued that such images make their subjects more accessible, that they introduce a new realism which allows the viewer
to identify with the subjects through imaginative devotion. Yet
this new "realism" cannot be allowed to obscure ideological readings according to which images of Joseph allowing an unruly child
to pull his beard promote the Franciscan ideal of humility. With
such an image, the potential gain in masculinity by the shifting of
one quality—such as age—is negated by the prominence or heap-
ing up of de-masculinizing qualities. Joseph's humble subordination could scarcely be more clearly stated than in a miniature by
the Master of the Dresden Prayer Book painted between about 1480

and 1490 (Fig. 4).[78] In this Flemish *Book of Hours*, the scene of
the Flight into Egypt sharply differentiates the humble, old Joseph
from the beautiful and self-absorbed young Mary. She concen-
trates on holding up the shimmering skirt of her expensive costume, while the task of carrying the infant is, most unusually, relegated to Joseph. This lack of dignity does not fit the patriarchal
masculinity that Gerson was constructing for Joseph.

Even when graced with a halo, as in the miniature of the Nativity from an early sixteenth-century *Book of Hours* now in the
Morgan Library (Fig. 5), Joseph can still be excluded from the Oedipal triangle of Symbolic Father, Symbolic Mother, and Ego. The rays
of divine light forming the apex of a triangle signify the presence
of God the Father and render Joseph's lantern somewhat irrelevant. The way he is silhouetted against the sky in Jean Bourdichon's
beautiful miniature, in contrast to the dark background behind
Mary and the child in the manger, works to place Joseph at the mar-
gin of the event.

Further, Joseph continues to be identified as a Jew, whether
through miserliness, costume, or distance from Mary and the child.
According to Brigitte Heublein, only in the course of the sixteenth
century do references to the Jewish Joseph and his identity with
the Old Covenant disappear.[79] Given the increasing anti-Judaism
of the late Middle Ages, Joseph's explicit Jewish identity surely
complicated any effort to present him as a model for a community
of Christian men.

For Ruth Mellinkoff such "belittling" portrayals are "due to
unresolved questions, such as whether or not Joseph should be
considered an Old Testament or a New Testament figure, whether
or not he could understand his role in salvation history, and
whether or not he was innately pious and holy or only a humble,
temporary servant of God."[80] I agree with Mellinkoff that such questions were unresolved in the fifteenth century, and I would emphasize that the symbolic field in which answers were posited was the
field of gender representation.

Striking evidence of the revision of Joseph's gender characteristics can be found in Maryan Ainsworth's x-radiographic study of a
painting by Gerard David now in the Cleveland Museum of Art.
David had adopted the Bridgittine iconography for the Nativity,
and produced a number of paintings in which both Joseph and
Mary kneel in adoration of the infant lying on the ground. Joseph,

wrinkled, balding, and grey-bearded, holds a small candle and shelters its flame, as in the *Nativity*, dated to the early 1480s, now in the Metropolitan Museum of Art, or in a painting of the same subject now in Budapest. As the underdrawing and x-radiographs demonstrate, the Cleveland painting had been based on the same type of Joseph. However, the present painting features a Joseph who is beardless and smooth-skinned, and whose hands meet in the same gesture of adoration as Mary's. Ainsworth considers the possibility that the revision was done in the sixteenth century, and that "the new owner was interested in superimposing another Joseph type at a time when the increased significance and resulting prominence of this figure responded to a growing cult of Saint Joseph."[81] A feast day was, in fact, assigned to Joseph by the Franciscan pope Sixtus IV (1471–84), though it was only a *festum simplex.*

Thus, Gerson had begun a campaign that would eventually transform the representation of Joseph into an "illustris patriarcha," a figure of power and authority, but that transformation could only slowly and with difficulty overwrite the existing constructions of Joseph. Not until the seventeenth century did Pope Gregory XV designate Joseph's feast day a holy day of obligation for the Universal Church.

Further, Gerson's commitment to gender hierarchy as crucial for order conflicted with the Conciliarist position he took at the Council of Constance. He had been championing the cause of Joseph for much of his career, even as his ideas about the power relationship between the pope and the Church were swinging back and forth. In his sermon to the Council on March 23, 1415, *Ambulate dum lux habetis,* Gerson spoke of "the Church as the Mystical Body of Christ, its indefectible Spouse; its infusion with life by the Holy Spirit; the possibility of divorcing itself from its 'secondary head', the Pope."[82] Gerson had reached this position of Conciliar supremacy over the papacy in reaction to events; as Morrall observes, he would have recoiled from it twenty years earlier.[83] A self-described conservative, Gerson's radicalism on this issue resulted in "noticeable inconsistencies" in his thought.[84] His decision to forward the cause of Joseph at the Council is part and parcel of those inconsistencies, for it involved him in a massive inconsistency with regard to gender hierarchy. Conciliarism meant the rule of the Church over the pope, that is, the *sponsa* over the *sponsus,* a position clearly in tension with Gerson's understanding of order between the genders. Gerson had argued that "Christ transmitted his supreme authority to the church as a community, not as an individual, and therefore general councils represent Christ," according to Antony Black,[85] but any attempt to follow through on the level of metaphor by gendering the Church as masculine would have run counter to the central metaphor of the marriage of *sponsus* and *sponsa*, Christ and the Church—both could not be masculine. But the position consistent with gender hierarchy, that the pope should rule over the Church as Joseph ruled over Mary, nullified Conciliarism. Yet this is the position Gerson enunciated at the end of his sermon. Perhaps the Conciliarists at the council recognized that Joseph would be a better symbol for the Papalists!

In Benedict Anderson's terminology, Gerson was imagining a community, a community of churchmen united under the patronage of Joseph.[86] He says at the end of his sermon: "Not that I want to recommend an increase in feasts for the folk who live by the labor of their hands—if for these people the number of feasts were fewer, then this council would be noted for its reforms—but I am speaking of such things to those in the religious life and about those in the religious life when I greatly desire that there should be a feast in celebration of the virginal marriage of Joseph and Mary or for his blessed departure."[87] The production of such an imagined community requires "representational labour" as Lesley Johnson puts it.[88] As we have already seen, Gerson's labor at Constance was doomed by his failure to synthesize his own ideas: "The Constance treatises are as far as an extremely subtle mind can go in effecting a synthesis between irreconcilable propositions; his failure to achieve the impossible might serve as an epitome of the dilemma which proved the downfall of the whole Conciliar movement."[89] But it is also worth considering that Gerson had no "other" against which to construct his Universal Church, for there was as yet no irreconcilable split within western Christianity. Later, in the context of the Reformation, papalism firmly triumphed, and took as its symbol Saint Joseph, a celibate male still especially venerated by Catholic churchmen.[90]

Figure 1.   Nativity, *Book of Hours.*
Bodleian Library, University of Oxford, MS. Douce 144, fol. 63

Figure 2. Nativity, *Hastings Hours.*
By permission of the British Library, Add. 54782, fol. 106v

Figure 3.   The Virgin Mary, Joseph, and Jesus.
Paris, Musée national du Moyen Age—Thermes et hôtel de Cluny, Cl. 15390

Figure 4.   Flight into Egypt, *Book of Hours.*
Collection of the J. Paul Getty Museum, Los Angeles, Ms 23, fols. 114v–115r

Figure 5.   Nativity, *Book of Hours.*
The Pierpont Morgan Library, New York, M. 732, fol. 31v

Notes

1. There is a large Gerson bibliography. For an overview of Gerson and his significance see the excellent introduction to *Jean Gerson: Early Works*, trans. and intro. Brian Patrick McGuire (Mahwah, N.J., 1998). For a magisterial synthesis of Gerson's attitudes toward women see chapter 7 of D. Catherine Brown, *Pastor and Laity in the Theology of Jean Gerson* (Cambridge, 1987), to which I am much indebted.

2. Brown, *Pastor and Laity*, 219. Brown refers to Gerson's sermon, "Poenitemini, contre la luxere," in volume 7, part 2 of the standard edition of Gerson's works: *Jean Gerson: Oeuvres complètes*, ed. Palemon Glorieux, 10 vols. (Paris, 1960–73), hereafter cited as *Oeuvres complètes* with relevant volume number.

3. Brown, *Pastor and Laity*, 219; Brown's translation is from the sermon, "Puer natus est" (*Oeuvres complètes*, 7:959).

4. ". . . every teaching of women, especially that expressed in solemn word or writing, is to be held suspect, unless it had been diligently examined, and much more than the teaching of men. Why? The reason is clear; because not only ordinary but divine law forbids such things. Why? Because women are too easily seduced, because they are too obstinately seducers, because it is not fitting that they should be knowers of divine wisdom" (Brown, *Pastor and Laity*, 223); Brown's translation is from *De examinatione doctrinarum*, written in 1423 (*Oeuvres complètes*, 9:468). For Gerson's doubts about Bridget see his *De probatione spirituum* in *Oeuvres complètes* 9. On this text see Paschal Boland, *The Concept of "discretio spirituum" in John Gerson's "De probatione spirituum" and "De distinctione verarum visionum a falsis"* (Washington, D.C., 1959). For an analysis of Gerson's distrust of female mystics see Dyan Elliott, "*Dominae* or *Dominatae?* Female Mysticism and the Trauma of Textuality," in *Women, Marriage, and Family in Medieval Christendom: Essays in Memory of Michael M. Sheehan, C.S.B.* ed. Constance M. Rousseau and Joel T. Rosenthal (Kalamazoo, 1998), 47–77.

5. Brown, *Pastor and Laity*, 223 (Brown's translation is from *De examinatione doctrinarum*, *Oeuvres complètes*, 9:467–68).

6. On these sculptures, called "Schreinmadonna" in German, see Renate Kroos, "'Gotes tabernakel': Zur Funktion und Interpretation von Schreinmadonnen," *Zeitschrift für Schweizerische Archäeologie und Kunstgeschichte* 43 (1986): 58–64; Corine Schleif, "Die Schreinmadonna im Diözesanmuseum zu Limburg: Ein verfemtes Bildwerk des Mittelalters," *Nassauische Annalen* 95 (1984): 39–54; Christoph Baumer, "Die Schreinmadonna," *Marian Literary Studies* 9 (1977): 239–72; Adelheid Brachert-von der Goltz, "Eine Schreinmadonna aus Kayserberg (Oberelsass)," *Schweizerisches Institut für Kunstwissenschaft*, Jahresbericht und Jahrbuch

(1966): 87–92; Walther Fries, "Die Schreinmadonna," in *Anzeiger des Germanischen Nationalmuseums* (Nürnberg 1928–29), 5–69; Alfred A. Schmid, "Die Schreinmadonna von Cheyres," in *Lebendiges Mittelalter: Festgabe für Wolfgang Stammler* (Freiburg/Schweiz, 1958), 130–62.

7. "Non enim propter aliam causam factae sunt imagines, nisi ad ostendendum simplicibus hominibus, qui non norunt Scripturam, quid credere debeant. Et propterea cavendum est, ne falsa aliqua accipiatur historia, quemamodum esset, perperam exponendo Scripturam. Haec dico partim propter quamdam Imaginem, quae est in Carmelities, et similes, quae in ventribus earum unam habent Trinitatem, veluti si tota Trinitas in Vergine Maria carnem assumpsisset humanam. Et quod admirabilius est, depicti sunt inferi, quorum nullus cernitur exitus. Nec video quare talia fiant opera. Mea namque sententia nulla in eis est pulchritudo, nec devotio, et possunt esse cause erroris et indevotionis" (Latin quotation from a sermon on the Nativity of the Virgin in Corine Schleif, "Die Schreinmadonna in Diözesanmuseum zu Limburg: Ein verfemtes Bildwerk des Mittelalters," *Nassauische Annalen* 95 [1984]: 48).

8. In the debate over the *Roman de la Rose*, Gerson indicts the *Rose* not only for its content, but especially for its visuality; he complains that the attractions of the *Rose* are "portrayed skilfully and lavishly in words and pictures, the more quickly to allure people into hearing, seeing, and holding fast to these things" (*La Querelle de la Rose: Letters and Documents*, trans. J. L. Baird and John R. Kane [Chapel Hill, N. C., 1978], 73). Later in the same treatise he castigates the *Rose* for its "dissolute, filthy, lecherous words, writings, and pictures" (77). For an edition of the French and Latin texts see Christine de Pizan, Jean Gerson, Jean de Montreuil, Gontier and Pierre Col, *Le Débat sur le Roman de la Rose*, edition critique, introduction, traductions, notes by Eric Hicks (1977; rpt. Geneva, 1996).

9. R. N. Swanson refers to Caroline Bynum's conclusions "that women mystics 'seem to have felt that they *qua* women were not only *also* but even *especially* saved in the Incarnation', and that the idea that womanhood signifies Christ's humanity was 'in some sense . . . literally true.'" "If such attitudes were shared generally among women," Swanson continues, "then the possible marginalisation of the male, and more particularly of the masculine, becomes a real issue. Among the rethinking which that demands is a re-examination of the relationship between men and Christianity" (R. N. Swanson, *Religion and Devotion in Europe, c. 1215–c. 1515* [Cambridge, 1995], 306).

10. For Gerson's efforts to end the Schism see John B. Morrall, *Gerson and the Great Schism* (Manchester, 1960).

11. Here Gerson was indicating his endorsement of Gregory XI's views on the subject; see Brown, *Pastor and Laity*, 223.

12. Rosemary Drage Hale, "Joseph as Mother: Adaptation and Appropriation in the Construction of Male Virtue," in *Medieval Mothering,* ed. John Carmi Parsons and Bonnie Wheeler (New York, 1996), 108. For an excellent, succinct formulation of Gerson's role in rehabilitating Joseph, see Clarissa Atkinson, *The Oldest Vocation: Christian Motherhood in the Middle Ages* (Ithaca, N. Y., 1991), 159–60.

13. For a still valuable overview of the cult of Joseph, which includes visual material, see Joseph Seitz, *Die Verehrung des hl. Joseph in ihrer geschichtlichen Entwicklung bis zum Konzil von Trient dargestellt* (Freiburg im Breisgau, 1908). For a recent treatment focused on visual material see Brigitte Heublein, *Der "verkannte" Joseph: Zur mittelalterliche Ikonographie des Heiligen im deutschen und niederländischen Kulturraum* (Weimar, 1998).

14. "The whole universe, in Gerson's thought, is ordered and reflects the order of the heavenly city. The heavens, the stars, indeed, all the elements of the earth together with the laws that govern them, speak of God's order" (Louis B. Pascoe, *Jean Gerson: Principles of Church Reform* [Leiden, 1973], 22).

15. Pascoe, *Jean Gerson,* 25; Pascoe continues, "Gerson, indeed, does not hesitate to call the pope the *primus hierarcha.* Through this hierarchical order and subordination, the church manifests itself as a visible image of the celestial kingdom."

16. ". . . he states that *Christianitas* can only be maintained by preserving the order characteristic of the heavenly kingdom" (Pascoe, *Jean Gerson,* 23).

17. Brown, *Pastor and Laity,* 216, quoting from "Diligite justiciam" (*Oeuvres complètes,* 7:605–606).

18. Brown, *Pastor and Laity,* 217, quoting "Poenitemini, de la chasteté conjugale" (*Oeuvres complètes,* 7:82); according to Brown, Gerson is quoting Hugh of St. Victor here.

19. Stephen Rigby offers a very clear summary of Parkin's theory: "In Parkin's view, Weber's theory of *social closure* offers a set of common concepts and a vocabulary with which to analyse all structured social inequalities, including those between classes, those within particular classes, and those between communal- and status-groups based on race, religion, or gender. For Parkin, all of these particular forms of social closure are 'different means of mobilising power for the purpose of engaging in distributive struggle.' Closure is thus the process by which social groups attempt to maximise their rewards and opportunities" ("Approaches to Pre-Industrial Social Structure," in *Orders and Hierarchies in Late Medieval and Renaissance Europe,* ed. Jeffrey Denton [Toronto, 1999], 13).

20. Pascoe, *Jean Gerson,* 39.

21. Ibid., 40.

22. See Max Lieberman, "Pierre d'Ailly, Jean Gerson et le culte de saint Joseph," *Cahiers de Joséphologie* 13 (1965): 227–72 and 14 (1966): 271–314.

23. "Ecclesiis universis, praesertim dedicatis in memoriam beatissimae et gloriosae semper Virginis Mariae" is dated August 17, 1413. For the text of the office Gerson composed, see "Officium sacrum in festivitate S. Ioseph cum officio missae et prosis" (*Oeuvres complètes*, 8:55–61).

24. Morrall, *Gerson and the Great Schism*, 94.

25. Ibid., 95.

26. "Jacob autem genuit Joseph" (*Oeuvres complètes*, 5:344–62).

27. This was apparently the first time Gerson had suggested that Joseph may have been sanctified in the womb, according to Otto Pfülf, "Die Verehrung der hl. Joseph in der Geschichte," *Stimmen aus Maria-Laach* 38 (1890): 159.

28. Gerson had made the general argument in his "Considérations sur saint Joseph": "Let us consider that each person is able to acquire his own nobleness in himself by virtuous operation and to be the beginning so that his successors should be reputed noble, according to what Tully said against Sallust; just as to the contrary a person of noble lineage is able to end the nobility in his person by vile sinfulness and evilness" (*Oeuvres complètes*, 7:71; my translation).

29. Ibid.

30. Beginning in the thirteenth century and with increased frequency in the fourteenth, these texts were translated and adapted in the European vernaculars. Some of these vernacular manuscripts were illustrated. For an overview see C. M. Kauffmann, "Art and Popular Culture: New Themes in the Holkham Bible Picture Book," in *Studies in Medieval Art and Architecture presented to Peter Lasko*, ed. David Buckton and T. A. Heslop (London, 1994), 46–69.

31. "At vero quia corpus Mariae fuit ipsius Joseph jure matrimoniali quo fit mutua translatio corporum viri ad mulierem et e contra, videamus si cum intelligentiae sobrietate dicere fas nobis sit quod ex corpore et carne Joseph natus est Jesus Christus. Et hoc dici forsitan posset nisi piarum aurium timeretur offensio," "Jacob autem," (*Oeuvres complètes*, 5:357; all translations from this sermon are my own).

32. "O dignitas incomparabilis ut mater Dei, regina coeli, domina mundi, appellare te dominum non indignum putaverit. Nescio sane, patres orthodoxi, quid hic amplius habeat mirabilis vel humilitas in Maria vel in Joseph sublimitas . . ." ("Jacob autem," *Oeuvre complètes*, 5:358).

33. "Considérations sur St Joseph," *Oeuvres complètes*, 7:66 (my translation). For a fascinating study of a twentieth-century Christian group, Women's Aglow, based on the doctrine of female submission to male au-

thority, see R. Marie Griffith, *God's Daughters: Evangelical Women and the Power of Submission* (Berkeley, 1997).

34. "Unde cum gratia, similiter et gloria naturam non tollat sed extollat et perficiat, recogitemus pia devotione quod si vinculo quodam naturalis obligationis quae consurgit filii ad matrem et matris ad sponsum suum et utriusque, scilicet filii et matris ad fidelissimum, vigilantissimum, et sedulum custodem et nutritium Joseph qui fuit caput Mariae, habens inde auctoritatem aliquam, principatum, dominationem vel imperium in Mariam sicut et Maria suo modo in filium suum Jesum iure naturalis maternitatis, quantus existimandus est justus ipse Joseph nunc in gloria et in coelis qui talis et tantus inventus est hic in miseria et in terris" (*Oeuvres complètes*, 7:66).

35. Although Gerson argues by analogy with Jerome's claim that Jesus was present at the death of Mary, he may also have been familiar with an apocryphal text, *The History of Joseph the Carpenter*, that purports to be the words of Jesus transcribed by the apostles as Jesus spoke to them on the Mount of Olives, and similarly describes the death of Joseph as an emotion-filled deathbed scene. It survives in a fifth-century Coptic version, and a Latin translation was known in western Europe by the fourteenth century. See Siegfried Morenz, ed. and trans., *Die Geschichte von Joseph dem Zimmerman* (Berlin, 1951).

36.
> " . . . etenim sic credere fas est
> Quod patrem Jesus et sponsum flevit morientem
> Virgo benigna suum. Fidi custodis amato.
> Procumbit lecto, complexans membra, pudicis
> Oscula dat labiis; mi vir, conclamat, abisne?
> Deseris et viduam passuram dira relinquis.
> Velle tamen Domini fiat; dilecte vale. Nil
> Ecce Jesus, timeas; placida te sede locabit.
> Protinus ipse Joseph pretiosa morte quievit."
>   ("Jacob autem," 5:356).

37. "Sane quatenus meritis, et intercessione tanti tamque potentis et imperiosi quodammodo patroni apud sponsam suam, de qua natus est Jesus qui vocatur Christus, reddatur Ecclesia unico viro vero et certo, Summo Pontifici sponso suo vice Christi" ("Jacob autem," 5:362).

38. See Brian Patrick McGuire's fascinating article on a sermon in which Gerson speaks in Bernard's voice: "Gerson took a line from the Song of Songs and commented on it in a way that Bernard himself might have done" (127). "The chancellor had decided to confront his audience as if he were the very voice of the saint, thus making the abbot of Clairvaux's life and doctrines much more vivid and immediate than they

would have been if expressed in the third person. 'Turn then for a little while your minds from me and think that it is Bernard himself speaking and not I'" (135) (Brian Patrick McGuire, "Gerson and Bernard: Languishing with Love," *Citeaux Commentarii Cistercienses* 46 [1995]: 127–56).

39. Rachel Fulton has shown that the Marian interpretation of the Song of Songs arose from the need for texts for the feast of her Assumption in "'Quae est ista quae ascendit sicut aurora consurgens?' The Song of Songs as the *Historia* for the Office of the Assumption," *Mediaeval Studies* 60 (1998): 55–122.

40. Peter Olivi, *Postilla super Mattheum*, cap 1, quest. 1.12, as quoted by Francis L. Filas, *The Man Closest to Jesus* (Boston, 1962), 498.

41. Judith M. Bennett, "Confronting Continuity," *Journal of Women's History* 9, no. 3 (Autumn 1997): 90.

42. A delegate from Cologne wrote in a letter of March 31, 1415: "The University of Paris is well situated with regard to the affairs of the Church and has a large audience. For in difficult matters, they are accustomed to consult its doctors and masters (of whom there are two hundred or more in Constance) and to follow their advice" (Universitatas Parisiensis bene se habet in negotiis Ecclesie et habet magnam audientiam. Solent enim in arduis doctores et magistros sue Universitatis Constantie existentes, .cc. in numero vel plures, congregare et de consilio eorum concludere). Quoted in Etienne Delaruelle, E. R. Labande, and Paul Ourliac, *L'Eglise au temps du Grand Schisme et de la crise conciliaire (1378–1449)*, 2 vols. Histoire de l'église depuis les origines jusqu'a nos jours 14 (Paris, 1962–64), vol. 1, 179.

43. Bonaventure, *In Vigilia Nat. Dom.*, sermo 11, *Opera*, 11:637–38, as quoted by Éphrem Longpré, "Saint Joseph et l'École franciscaine du XIIIe siècle," in *Le patronage de Saint Joseph: Actes du Congrès d'études tenu à l'Oratoire Saint-Joseph, Montréal, 1er–9 aôut 1955* (Montreal and Paris, 1956), 227.

44. "Decens etiam fuit ut tali homini nuberet triplici ex causa: scilicet ratione generis, ratione fidelitatis et ratione paupertatis. Ratione generis, quia erat de tribu Juda et de semine David et propinquue Beatae Virginis et per ipsum descripta est genealogia Christi, quae non debet per foeminas describi, sicut Hieronymus super Matthaeum dicit. Secunda ratio est, quia fuit vir castus et justus, sicut dicit Evangelium; et ut esset Virgini in solatium et in testimonium eunti in Aegyptum, datus est ei a Deo in virum. Tertia ratio est propter paupertatem quia Christus super omnia venit confundere superbiam, non voluit vocari filius regis sed magis filius fabri. In quo ostenditur Christi humilitas et etiam ipsius Virginis gloriosae et confusa est mundanorum superbia" (IV *Sent.*, d. 30, a. 1, q. 2, *Opera*, vol. IV, p. 710, quoted in Longpré 226–27. See also

Joseph Duserre, "Les origines de la dévotion à Saint Joseph," *Cahiers de Josephologie* 1 (1953): 23–54, 169–96 and 2 (1954): 5–30; Marjory Bolger Foster, *The Iconography of St. Joseph in Netherlandish Art, 1400–1500,* doctoral dissertation, University of Kansas, 1979.

45. Bonaventure, *In Vigilia Nat. Dom.*, sermo 11, *Opera,* 11:637–38, as quoted by Longpré, 227.

46. Blaine Burkey, "The Feast of St. Joseph: A Franciscan Bequest," *Cahiers de Joséphologie* 19 (1971): 647–80.

47. "Et considera super omnes alias illam benedictam familiam paruam, sed ualde excelsam pauperem et humilem uitam ducentem. Felix senex Ioseph querebat quod poterat de arte lignaminis" (15.160–64; M. Stallings-Taney, ed., *Johannis de Caulibus. Meditaciones vite Christi olim S. Bonaventuro attributae.* Corpus Christianorum. Continuatio Mediaevalis CLIII [Turnholt, 1997]). Stallings-Taney dates the text *c.* 1346–*c.* 1364.

48. See, for example, the miniature on fol. 43v of Paris, BNF, ital. 115 (14th century), reproduced in Isa Ragusa and Rosalie B. Green, *Meditations on the Life of Christ. An Illustrated Manuscript of the Fourteenth Century* (Princeton, N.J., 1961), 76. In a visual expansion of the text, which simply reports that while they were in Egypt Joseph worked as a woodworker, the miniature shows him wielding an adze to hollow out a trough as two men approach him. The caption reports that the two men want to buy the kneading-trough. Joseph is thus a maker of humble items used in the household, not a fine craftsman.

49. See the sequence of illustrations on fol. 12r of the *Holkham Bible* (BL Add. 47682; *c.* 1320–30) that show Joseph's doubt about Mary's pregnancy and its resolution. He digs with an iron-shod spade while listening to gossip about Mary, and has it with him as a kind of attribute when the angel speaks to him and when he subsequently apologizes to Mary. The spade is so basic to Joseph's identity in this manuscript that it even accompanies him to Bethlehem (fol. 12v). See W. O. Hassall, *The Holkham Bible Picture Book* (London, 1954) for reproductions. Aimed at a lay audience, this manuscript indicates that the representation of Joseph as peasant circulated among the "rich gent" (fol. 1r); see Kauffmann, "Art and Popular Culture," who concludes that "we are dealing with a merchant-class audience in a large town, and London remains the likeliest" (64).

50. See Zsuzsa Urbach, " 'Dominus possedit me . . .' (Prov. 8, 22): Beitrag zur Ikonographie des Josephzweifels," *Acta Hist. Art. Hung.* 20 (1974): 199–266.

51. See Joseph L. Baird and Lorrayne Y. Baird, "Fabliau Form and the Hegge *Joseph's Return*," *The Chaucer Review* 8, no. 2 (1993): 159–69; Martin W. Walsh, "Divine Cuckold/Holy Fool: The Comic Image of Joseph in the English 'Troubles' Plays," *Proceedings of the 1985 Harlaxton*

Symposium, ed. W.M. Ormrod (Woodbridge, Suffolk, 1986), 278–97; Philip C. Deasy, *St. Joseph in the English Mystery Plays,* doctoral dissertation, Catholic University of America, 1937.

52. Mellinkoff disagrees with those who interpret the representation of Joseph's drinking as a simple indicator that the scene was understood as humble: "the conception, if humble, is humble in a denigrating sense, because it indicates that the 'humble' Joseph is a peasant boor who drinks too much. Even a haloed version of Joseph shown drinking his fill does not, in my view, rescue Joseph from belittling connotations" (Ruth Mellinkoff, *Outcasts: Signs of Otherness in Northern European Art of the Late Middle Ages,* 2 vols. [Berkeley, 1993], 1:226).

53. "Mirum est, quod tam pulchra mulier, devota et faceta, obprobria et verbera sustinet tam patienter ab illo antiquo Joseph!" (*Die Akten des Kanonisationsprozesses Dorotheas von Montau von 1394 bis 1521,* Forschungen und Quellen zur Kirchen- und Kulturgeschichte Ostdeutschlands, vol. 12, ed. Richard Stachnik [Cologne and Vienna, 1978], 390, as quoted by Dyan Elliott, *Spiritual Marriage: Sexual Abstinence in Medieval Wedlock* [Princeton, N.J., 1993], 254).

54. Elliott, *Spiritual Marriage,* 254, quoting *Vita Dorotheae* 3.9, 124–25.

55. On this subject in the visual arts see Alison G. Stewart, *Unequal Lovers: A Study of Unequal Couples in Northern Art* (New York, 1977); for the special case of God the Father and the Virgin Mary, see my "The Maternal Behavior of God: Divine Father as Fantasy Husband," in *Medieval Mothering,* ed. John Carmi Parsons and Bonnie Wheeler (New York, 1996), 77–99.

56. For Stanton's characterization see "*La genealogye comence:* Kinship and Difference in the *Queen Mary Psalter,*" *Studies in Iconography* 17 (1996): 178. For a color reproduction of this miniature, which is on fol. 151r of the *Queen Mary Psalter,* see Stanton's "From Eve to Bathsheba and Beyond: Motherhood in the Queen Mary Psalter," in *Women and the Book: Assessing the Visual Evidence,* ed. Lesley Smith and Jane H.M. Taylor (London, 1996), colorplate 7. It is worth noting that Stanton assigns ownership of this manuscript to Isabella, queen of Edward II of England and that Isabella's library also contained Franciscan service books. Stanton further points out that Isabella was a patron of the church of the Grey Friars in London; she was buried there, as were several of her Franciscan confessors. Thus it seems quite possible that the humble Joseph of this miniature was influenced by the Franciscan construction of Joseph. See Stanton's "Isabella of France and Her Manuscripts, 1308–1330," in *Capetian Women,* ed. Kathleen Nolan and John Carmi Parsons (New York, forthcoming).

57. See Leopold Schmidt, "'Sankt Joseph kocht ein Müselein': Zur Kindlbreiszene in der Weihnachtskunst des Mittelalters," in *Europäische*

Sachkultur des Mittelalters. Gedenkschrift aus Anlass des zehnjährigen Bestehens des Instituts für mittelalterliche Realienkunde Österreichs (Österreiche Akademie des Wissenschaften. Philosophisch-Historische Klasse. Sitzungsberichte, 374); Band, Veröffentlichungen des Institute für Mittelalterliche Realienkunde Österreichs, Bd. 4 (Vienna, 1980), 143–66.

58. For this performance in Cologne *c.* 1547 see Bernd Neumann, *Geistliches Schauspiel im Zeugnis der Zeit: Zur Aufführung mittelalterlicher religiöser Dramen im deutschen Sprachgebiet* (Munich, 1987), 2:921–22 [No. 3754]. For a translation of the relevant scene, which the translator characterizes as "slapstick," see Stephen K. Wright, "Joseph as Mother, Jutta as Pope: Gender and Transgression in Medieval German Drama," *Theatre Journal* 51 (1999): 157, n. 17.

59. As Mellinkoff notes (*Outcasts* 1:225), miserliness was sometimes attributed to Joseph in the drama as well. See Mellinkoff for relevant illustrations.

60. In a chapter devoted to headgear, Mellinkoff discusses portrayals of Joseph wearing a Jew's hat (*Outcasts*, 1:79–82). Representations in which the representation of Joseph as a Jew appears to be a deliberate choice can be found from the beginning of the twelfth century.

61. See Heublein, *Der "verkannte" Joseph*, 23–44, for the gesture as meditative, and 73, as well as figure 42, for Joseph as personification.

62. See Willis Johnson, "The Myth of Jewish Male Menses," *Journal of Medieval History* 24, no. 3 (1998): 273–95, esp. 286; Johnson cites Peter Biller, "Views of Jews from Paris Around 1300: Christian or 'Scientific'," in *Christianity and Judaism*, ed. Diana Wood (Studies in Church History 29 [1992]), 187–207, esp. 192).

63. The commentary appears to be from the early fourteenth century, according to Johnson, "Myth," 294. He cites it from Helen R. Lemay, *Women's Secretes: A Translation of Pseudo-Albertus Magnus's de Secretis Mulierum with Commentaries* (Albany, N.Y., 1992), 74.

64. "E gli sciocchi dipintori el dipingono vecchio maninconoso e colla mano alla gota, come s'elli avessi dolore o maninconia" (quoted and translated by Franco Mormando, *The Preacher's Demons: Bernardino of Siena and the Social Underworld of Early Renaissance Italy* [Chicago, 1999], 32, 250).

65. A paper on this subject was delivered at Columbia University's Branner Forum and at the NEH Summer Institute, "Sex and Gender in the Middle Ages."

66. Judith Butler, *Bodies That Matter: On the Discursive Limits of Sex* (New York, 1993), 243.

67. Ibid.

68. "His figure is contrasted with the grandeur of the Incarnation, in which Mary is the central figure and the embodiment of the greatest

mystery of all" (Hans Nieuwdorp, "The Antwerp-Baltimore Polyptych: A Portable Altarpiece Belonging to Philip the Bold, Duke of Burgundy," in Henk van Os, *The Art of Devotion in the Late Middle Ages in Europe 1300–1500* [Princeton, N.J., 1994], 140).

69.   Steven F. Kruger, "The Bodies of Jews in the Late Middle Ages," in *The Idea of Medieval Literature: New Essays on Chaucer and Medieval Culture in Honor of Donald R. Howard*, ed. James M. Dean and Christian Zacher (Newark, Del., 1992), 301–23. Note, however, that Johnson, "Myth," has shown that the idea on which Kruger partly bases his argument, that of the menstruating Jewish man, was not a medieval idea.

70.   Freedman, chapter 7, "Peasant Bodies, Male and Female."

71.   Vern L. Bullough, "On Being a Male in the Middle Ages," in *Medieval Masculinities: Regarding Men in the Middle Ages*, ed. Clare A. Lees (Minneapolis, 1994), 43.

72.   This illustration is on fol. 42v in a fifteenth-century French manuscript containing the *Livre des Propriétés des Choses* (Paris, BNF fr. 134). For a reproduction see *L'Enfance*, p. 17. In another manuscript of this text also from fifteenth-century France (BNF fr. 22531) the youth seduces a woman and the mature man counts his money (see Elizabeth Sears, *The Ages of Man: Medieval Interpretations of the Life Cycle* [Princeton, N.J., 1986], fig. 67. Obviously the Joseph of this period has more in common with the mature man.

73.   See fol. 336v of the fifteenth-century French manuscript of *Politiques, Economiques, et Ethiques d'Aristote* (Paris, BNF fr. 204), illustrated in *L'Enfance*, p. 95.

74.   Brown, *Pastor and Laity*, 2.

75.   Swanson, *Religion and Devotion*, 308; Swanson points to the cult of Joseph as one of the resulting developments.

76.   For an illustration in color see *The Hastings Hours*, preface and commentary by D. H. Turner (London, 1983).

77.

> Haa, bonne gens, je suis vieulx.
>
> La vierge seroit bien perdue
>
> D'avoir telle barbe chenue. (lines 1927–29)

For an edition see *The Passion de Semur*, edited with an introduction and notes by Lynette Muir, Leeds Medieval Studies 3 (Leeds, 1981).

78.   On this manuscript, known as the *Crohnin-La Fontaine Hours*, see the report of acquisitions in *The J. Paul Getty Museum Journal* 15 (1987): 172–74.

79.   Heublein, *Der "verkannte" Joseph*, 84.

80.   Mellinkoff, *Outcasts*, 1:222.

81.   Maryan W. Ainsworth, *Gerard David: Purity of Vision in an Age of Transition* (New York, 1998), 115.

82. Morrall, *Gerson and the Great Schism*, 96.

83. Morrall summarizes his impression of the treatises Gerson wrote during the Council of Constance: "The attempt to build an irrefragable theory of Conciliar supremacy at the Papacy's expense was the only permanent solution to the problem which Gerson could envision. The development of events had driven him to this position, from which he would have recoiled twenty years earlier" (*Gerson and the Great Schism*, 110).

84. "Gerson himself was unwilling to face the fact of his new radicalism. Like most innovators, he saw himself as a conservative. He is even far from admitting himself to be anti-Papal; for him the Papacy is of Divine institution and cannot 'lege stante' be permitted to disappear from its rightful place in Church government. At the same time, his desire to place the Council in clear superiority to the Papacy makes him reduce Papal power to a point where, as he admits, the question of the necessity of the institution might legitimately be raised. His efforts to meet this difficulty are hesitant and unconvincing, and the resulting tension between conservatism and radicalism in his thought is responsible for noticeable inconsistencies" (Morrall, *Gerson and the Great Schism*, 110).

85. Antony Black, *Political Thought in Europe, 1250–1450* (Cambridge, 1992), 171.

86. Benedict Anderson, *Imagined Communities: Reflections on the Origin and Spread of Nationalism* (1983; rev. ed. London, 1991).

87. "Non quod multiplicationem festivitatum apud vulgus quod de labore manuum vivere habet suadeamus; esset utinam apud tales hujusmodi numerus festivitatum minor, sicut in reformatione hic in concilio notatum est; sed apud ecclesiasticos de et ecclesiasticis talia loquimur dum de celebritate virginalis conjugii Joseph cum Maria vel de ipsius felici transitu fieri solemnitatem exoptamus" ("Jacob autem," 5:362).

88. With reference to Benedict Anderson's definition of the nation as an "imagined political community," Johnson explains, "The resonance of 'imagined' here is not 'not real' but constructed, produced: the nation is a construct which requires representational labour, is produced in and by representational work of some kind because this notion of community must be larger than any individual could experience directly" (Lesley Johnson, "Imagining Communities: Medieval and Modern," in *Concepts of National Identity in the Middle Ages*, ed. Simon Forde, Lesley Johnson, and Alan V. Murray, Leeds Texts and Monographs New Series 14 [Leeds, 1995], 6).

89. Morrall, *Gerson and the Great Schism*, 111.

90. Joseph was the patron of Vatican II. During that Council, "the bishops debated the question of whether or not they would petition the Pope to put the name of St. Joseph in the Canon of the Mass. The Pope

was following the discussion by television in his office and he immedi-
ately sent down a message. He said don't bother with the debate. Put his
name in immediately. So the name of Joseph went immediately into the
Canon of the Mass" (Cardinal Wright, "St. Joseph and Collegiality," in
San José en los XV primeros siglos de la iglesia. Actas del Simposio
Internacional en el primer centario de la proclamación de San José como
Patrono de la Iglesia Universel [Roma, 29 noviembre–6 diciembre 1970];
published as an entire volume of *Estudios Josefinos. Revista Dirigida por
Carmelitas Descalzos* 25 [nos. 49–50 (Enero-Diciembre, 1971)], 10).

CHAPTER FOUR

Catholic Communities and Their Art

Annabel Patterson

To use the phrase "Catholic Community" immediately summons up the commanding figure of John Bossy, whose 1976 study, *The English Catholic Community,* was a magisterial work of socio-religious history—extraordinary in its chronological range, from the later sixteenth century through the middle of the nineteenth—and heavily buttressed with statistics. The effect of these social historians' tactics was to free the topic from ideological constraints, removing the odor of bias or religious special pleading. Bossy began by remarking that:

> The English Catholic community has bred some great historians, but they have not contributed much to its own history. Their reluctance is understandable, but a pity; for it has left the community uneasily related to its past, uncertain where to look for it and what to make of it, embarrassed or over-devout, unable to draw on the kind of sustaining tradition which, whatever else he may lack, a Catholic ought presumably to have at his disposal.[1]

Bossy's goal, therefore, was to treat the English Catholic community like any other sociologically distinct and traceable group. For his purposes, however, it did not come into existence until 1570, two years after the creation of the Jesuit seminary at Douai (or, one might add, the very year of Elizabeth's excommunication by the pope). The year 1570 was Bossy's *terminus a quo* because it marked a change of attitude on the part of English Catholics; if not the assumption that the Reformation was here to stay, at least the acceptance of temporary minority status, and for the foreseeable future a battle of wits, a game of chess and sometimes of cat and mouse.

Bossy, however, departed from his major predecessor, David Mathew,[2] in defining English Catholics during this period as *not* a minority but a community because "a minority is by definition one of a pair; a community may be one of several." For by 1570, the English, in his view, were "divided for religious purposes not into Protestants and Catholics but into Anglicans, Presbyterians, Independents, Baptists, Fifth-monarchy men, Quakers, Unitarians, Methodists of various colours, Jews and a good deal more" (p. 5). Each of such groups either has or presumably could have its own social historian.

Actually, it would be more accurate to call Bossy's book *The English Catholic Communities* in the plural, for it gradually unfolds a series of different Catholic communities, not all of which were on good terms with the others. First come the groups of young Englishmen, often selected for their intelligence, sent to be trained as Catholics at Douai or to similar continental institutions. The poet Robert Southwell, for example, went to Douai at fifteen, from there to the Jesuit College of Clermont in Paris, and from there to the Roman and English Colleges in Rome. Those who returned from these schools as missionaries formed different communities again, divided between the Jesuits, who were comparatively few, and the so-called secular priests, by far the majority. The seculars, men like John Mush or Christopher Bagshaw, deeply resented the hold that the Jesuit minority had over the actual organization of the mission during its oversight by Robert Parsons and Henry Garnet, and by the appointment from Rome of the Archpriest George Blackwell. Then there were the Catholic gentry of Elizabeth's era, like Sir Thomas Tresham, in whose interest it was to encourage toleration of a small number of Catholic clergy who could minister to their families, and could therefore not be seen as dangerous to the regime. And by the time Bossy enters the seventeenth century, he begins to divide the Catholic gentry into ever more complicated regional subsets, with certain common features. Local communities, unsurprisingly, tended to be clustered around important Catholic families, especially in the North, whose servants and tenants became part of the ideological unit. Within the family the matriarch held extraordinary importance as a center of faith and discipline, often in defiance of her husband, but also because women were exempted from the full force of the penalties for recusancy; but for Bossy the true galvanic center of the Catholic family was the missionary priest.

What Bossy did not quite say, perhaps because to mention it would again raise from the grave the ghosts of indignation, is that English academic culture, and more broadly Anglo-American academic culture, has been for centuries consciously or unconsciously anti-Catholic in its choice of subjects for study; less so perhaps among historians proper than in my own discipline and especially in the field now referred to as Early Modern, where over and over again classes of undergraduates containing a fair proportion of young people born into Catholic families are confronted by, and expected to admire, authors like Luther or Machiavelli or Petrarch or Milton, or, as more complicated instances, Edmund Spenser and John Donne. In the last decade some strong voices have been heard protesting this *de facto* imbalance. Eamon Duffy's provocative account of popular resistance to the Reformation in England began in the late Middle Ages but carried its thesis—"of weary obedience to unpopular measures"—through to the Elizabethan Injunctions of 1559.[3] And Arthur Marotti's study of the cultural importance of Edmund Campion and Robert Southwell begins with the following challenge to orthodox opinion:

> English nationalism rests on a foundation of anti-Catholicism. In the sixteenth and seventeenth centuries . . . Roman Catholicism, especially in its post-Tridentine, Jesuit manifestations was cast as the hated and dangerous antagonist, most fearfully embodied in a papacy that claimed the right to depose monarchs. . . . A vocabulary of anti-Catholicism or anti-Popery was developed . . . becoming immersed finally in the post-1688 era in a Whig narrative of English history.[4]

Implicitly, Marotti's narrative extends into the present and rebukes those whose preferences for Protestant poetry have excluded that of the Jesuit Southwell from the canon,[5] a word which in these circumstances acquires more irony than usual. Southwell, who was executed at Tyburn in 1595, on a charge of treason—

treason having been extended to cover the crime of returning to England as an ordained priest of the Church of Rome—was beatified in 1929. Of course there is a large body of scholarship, usually by Catholics, devoted to figures like Campion and Southwell, or to the history of anti-Catholic prejudice in the past,[6] but Marotti initiates a dialogue with the assumptions of both older and newer scholars who, with only the slightest of qualifications, have bought into the triumphalist stories of English nationalism, Elizabethan justice, or the dangers inherent in crypto-catholicism under the various Stuarts. Among the last of these I must, especially on account of *Early Modern Liberalism,* count myself.

What follows is not exactly an act of reparation. Indeed, at moments I may sound as though I am reinstantiating anti-Catholicism in an insidious new form, or at least under a new heading, though I have tried to prune my vocabulary of any unconscious stigmatics. My focus here is on something entirely excluded from Bossy's investigations, and only incidentally touched upon by Duffy and Marotti: the role of the visual arts in consoling, consolidating, and even creating English Catholic communities at various stages of their history. In Duffy's study, of course, the shifting fortunes of English iconoclasm are a continuous theme; so that in 1559, as he describes it, ordinary parishioners "had seen all this before":

> the books and images burned, the altars stripped, and demolished, the vestments sold for cushions and bed-hangings. That destruction had had to be reversed [under Mary], with great difficulty and at enormous cost, and it was the rank and file of the parish who had borne the brunt. Now the newly acquired Roods and patronal statues . . . which Marian archdeacons had demanded from them, were to be once more pitched into wheelbarrows and trundled to the fire. (p. 571)

Duffy cites rich evidence of cunning and comic foot-dragging, the burying rather than the destruction of images, and the equally reversible strategy of whitewashing sacred pictures.

At the other end of the scale, the creative end, Marotti reestablishes Southwell's poetry as a form of sacred art written under huge stress to the ends of Catholic solidarity, and treated by the Catholic community as somewhere between a manifesto and a reliquary. But parenthetically he draws our attention to visual manifestos.

Frescoes of the English martyrdoms were painted on the walls of the English College in Rome;[7] and, in a Catholic re-appropriation of the strategy devised by John Foxe, the gruesome visual representation of specific executions, one of Southwell's colleagues, Richard Verstegan, produced in 1587 an illustrated account of the persecution of Catholics, from More and Fisher through to the execution of Mary, queen of Scots (Figs. 1 and 2).[8] Verstegan divides Protestant persecution of Catholics into four sections; Henrician, Huguenot, Belgian, and Elizabethan; and for the Elizabethan section his *terminus a quo* is also the year 1570.

My focus here, however, is not on the theatricalization of violence by opposite camps, but rather on two other art forms not usually connected: the first is sacred art itself, and its peculiar status in an age of English iconoclasm; the second is the portrait. I propose that Catholic communities learned to use the portrait as a partial substitute for other icons supportive of their belief. Of course in this they were not unique; the ideological role of the portrait, both in sixteenth-century Germany and England, in defining an international Protestant community, especially of scholars, is also beginning to be understood. But here I want to make the suggestion that the role assigned by Bossy to the missionary priest—the role of defining and consolidating the Catholic community—could also be played, in a less explicit but hardly less profound manner—by the early modern portrait painter.

I am lucky to be able to follow the initiative of a brilliant article by Clark Hulse on portraits of Sir Thomas More and his family, which, *pace* Bossy's chronological boundary but in line with his focus on the family, eventually constituted a small and embattled Catholic community. The family of More was first rendered an icon by Hans Holbein at a stage well before More became embroiled in the politics of the royal divorce and separation from Rome, when Catholicism was still the national religion; so that nothing much need be made of the art historical discovery that Holbein for this purpose secularized a composition he had used in 1526 for and of the Meyer family in the "Darmstadt Madonna," where the family members are grouped around and radiate from the Madonna and Child in the top center.[9] The original Holbein painting no longer exists, but in the seventeenth century it was acquired by Thomas Howard, second earl of Arundel, a connection that, as we will see, links a Henrician Catholic community to a Caroline one. Holbein's drawing of the More family for Erasmus (Fig. 3) has survived to tell us what the painting would have looked like. Hulse explains that it shows, from left to right, More's daughter Elizabeth Dauncey, his foster daughter Margaret Giggs, later Clement, his father Sir John More, Anne Cresacre his daughter-in-law, More himself in the compositional center, his son John More, his fool Henry Patenson, his youngest daughter Cecily Heron, his eldest and favorite daughter Margaret Roper, and his wife Alice. One might add a few other observations; first, that the placing of Margaret, his favorite daughter, closest to the spectator and in a semi-kneeling position, suggests the patronal or donor position of adoration, which is here redirected toward her father. Second, the design now secularized is patriarchal, rather than matriarchal; and third, that the drawing emphatically interprets the portrait as a scene of reading. All of the women are holding books, though Elizabeth Dauncey's is hard to see, being under her arm and closed. Margaret Giggs bends forward to show More Sr. something in hers; and Thomas More Jr. has one too. At their feet Holbein has sketched in several more lying on the floor.[10] Fourth, an item which will gather significance as this essay proceeds, Dame Alice is ostentatiously wearing a crucifix to balance More's badge of office. And lastly, almost above More's head[11] and very prominent in the design is a clock, which cannot but signify, even in 1527 when the drawing was made, human mortality, to which both genealogy and the humanist cult of the book provide comforting answers.

Hulse suggests that the original painting, perhaps initially sequestered with the rest of More's estate after his execution, must have temporarily passed back into family hands, which allowed for it to be copied, or rather adapted, in the 1590s. He shows that there were two separate versions made for the family by Rowland Lockey, the first either for Thomas Roper, the son of William and Margaret Roper, or for Thomas More II, the son of John More and Ann Cresacre; the second (Fig. 4) certainly for Thomas II, since the entire composition was shifted to the left, so as to permit the inclusion of *his* family. Thus in the second copy the centrality of the cult figure, More himself, is conceptually subordinated to his descendants, the immediate guardians of his legend. As Hulse shrewdly observes, this enshrining of the legend of More within his family connoted a broader defiance:

> The perpetuation of the More family is the perpetuation of a central element of the Roman Catholic Church in England. John More the younger was imprisoned. Cecily Heron's husband was executed. Thomas More II was himself a reluctant recusant who after years of quietism reasserted his Catholicism, suffered in prison from 1582 to 1586, and remained under surveillance when the painting was executed. (p. 216)

But we might also note that the scene of reading as such has vanished; that the balance between patriarchy and matriarchy seems to have shifted back in favor of the latter; and that the symbolic clock now competes with a portrait within the portrait, the image of Anne Cresacre, also emphatically wearing a crucifix around her neck, which by the 1590s was an open statement of recusancy. Mary Scrope, Thomas II's wife, also wears a somewhat less obvious version of the same symbol.

Catholic defiance or resistance seem occasionally to have been not merely a subtext but the rationale for portraiture. When in 1586 Anthony Babington was conspiring with his young band of fellow Catholics to remove Elizabeth from the throne and place Mary, Queen of Scots upon it instead, he commissioned portraits of himself and his fellow conspirators, with his own inscribed with a motto that bound the group together: "Quos mihi sunt Comites, quos ipsa Pericula ducunt." (These are my companions, whom Danger herself commands.) As Lorne Campbell discovered, Babington had planned to send a painter to Wales to complete the series, and intended to keep them "as a memorial of so worthy an act as attempting her majesty's person," but the portraits were seized along with the conspirators, and exhibited, significantly *not* in a group but separately throughout London, as a badge of their shame.[12]

John Donne was descended from another branch of the More family, not shown in these family portraits, but equally important for the idea of extended Catholic family as Catholic community. Donne's grandfather was the Tudor writer John Heywood, who had married Joan Rastell, herself the daughter of John Rastell and Elizabeth More, Sir Thomas More's sister. In *Pseudo-martyr*, Donne's first engagement in religious controversy on the side of the official Jacobean church and against the Jesuits, he made an awkward apology for his leaving the community into which he had been born:

> as I am a Christian, I have beene ever kept awake in a medita-
> tion of Martyrdome, by being derived from such a stock and
> race, as, I believe, no family, (which is not of farre larger extent,
> and greater branches,) hath endured and suffered more in their
> persons and fortunes, for obeying the Teachers of Romane Doc-
> trine, then it hath done.[13]

In a diagram of Donne's lineage, Dennis Flynn has demonstrated that no fewer than thirteen of his family connections, excluding More himself but including Donne's brother Henry, died either in prison or in exile for their Roman Catholic beliefs.[14] Donne him-self was deeply invested in portraits—of himself—a sad deflation of the idea of the cult image, half sacred, half secular, that por-traits of More, no less than those of Luther and Melanchthon, had by this time become. But throughout his life he seems to have been irresistibly drawn to the world of sacred images, and by the end of his career he had, at least in relation to the issue of icono-clasm, swerved back dramatically into the community from which, whether from strategic reasons or genuine conviction or both, he had in *Pseudo-martyr* publicly cut himself off.

Since the last five years of Donne's life as a dignitary of the Anglican church were presided over by Charles I, he can serve here as a link between the Henrician and Elizabethan Catholic com-munities and those of the Caroline era, and a transition from Hol-bein and his copyists to Van Dyck. In 1625, the year of Charles's accession, Catholic observers of the English political scene un-doubtedly acquired new hope. Not only had the new king married a Roman Catholic French queen, but, perhaps even more signifi-cantly, he made the Arminian Richard Montagu his chaplain in 1625 in defiance of parliamentary protest. In July 1627 he signified his disapproval of the moderately Calvinist Archbishop George Abbot by suspending him from all duties for refusing to license the Arminian cleric Robert Sibthorpe's *Apostolike Obedience*, origi-nally a sermon invoking support for Charles's forced loan. While in the same year the king also expressed displeasure at the queen's ostentatious displays of Catholic piety (visiting places of Catholic martyrdom such as Tyburn, for example) by dismissing, on July 31, most of her French retinue and priests. By autumn, with the help of Daniel Nys in Venice and Endymion Porter at home, he was already engaged in purchasing the great art collection of the dukes of Mantua,[15] a collection that included eleven "portraits" by Titian of Roman emperors, paintings by Andrea del Sarto, Correggio, Giulio Romano, Tintoretto, and a Raphael Madonna. A significant shift in the culture had begun, whereby the Caroline court not only became a locus of Catholic worship, albeit confined to the queen's chapel, but a locus of art that had itself been produced in and for Catholic sensibilities. How these developments were to be reconciled with the official iconoclasm of the English Church is a question with which the admirers of Charles I's connoisseurship have not often concerned themselves.

The issue of iconoclasm had in fact been quite an important part of the Richard Montagu affair; for although one cannot tell this from the parliamentary protests about his publications, one of Montagu's objectives had been to carve out a new centrist position between the Roman Catholic doctrine on images and strict Calvinist or Puritan iconomachy. Montagu had included in *A New Gagg for an Old Goose* (1624) several pages of what he probably conceived as a Lutheran defense of images, but which can equally be read as a defense of Counter-Reformation practice:

> Unto Christians they are not unlawful, for civil uses: nor utterly in all manner of religious imployment. The pictures of Christ, the blessed Virgin, and Saints may be had, had in houses, set up in Churches: the Protestants use them: they despight them not: Respect and honour may be given unto them: the Protestants doe it: and use them for helps of piety, in rememoration, and more effectual representing of the Prototype. (p. 318)

The following year, stung by a storm of criticism that his supposedly centrist position was in fact "arminianism" if not outright popery, Montagu had returned to the issue in *Apello Caesarem*, which had been read and approved for publication by James I shortly before his death; but the Caesar to whom it was now dedicated was Charles I. Montagu declared, among other things, that the strict iconoclasm of the Elizabethan Book of Homilies should now be understood historically, as an over-reaction:

> Our Predecessors and Fathers coming late out of Popery, living neere unto Papists and Popish times, conversing with them, having beene nuzzled and brought up amongst them . . . therefore . . . they spake thus vehemently, and indeed *hyperbolically* against [images]. (p. 263)

The iconographical or iconoclastic debate could not, surely, be completely insulated from the royal art collections. In 1628–29 parliamentary government collapsed, to be replaced with eleven years of Personal Rule and art acquisition. And in 1632, with the arrival of Van Dyck in London, there began to be produced, with extraordinary speed and brilliance, an art that celebrated Caroline rule in the same iconographical language that Van Dyck had been using to promote the Roman Catholic leadership of Europe. Van Dyck's new iconography served more than the ideological needs of Charles I; its embrace was extended, perhaps deliberately, to the English recusant community. It should not be forgotten that Van Dyck had in 1628 enrolled in the Sodalitedt van de Bejaerde Jongmans, a Jesuit confraternity of bachelors in Antwerp; and that his brother, Canon Theodore van Dyck, was offered, but apparently refused, a position in Henrietta Maria's religious household.

It appears, however, that Van Dyck had created some of his English images a good deal earlier, during his first visit to England in 1620, and that these early portraits prognosticate in more ways than one the program he would develop in the later 1630s. I refer first to his recently identified portrait of George Gage (Fig. 5). The portrait is intriguing both formally and ideologically. A group portrait inexplicable by the rank of the sitters, it suggests instead the theme of art connoisseurship, since Gage is shown in conversation with two men, one a Negro, who are evidently displaying the merits of a small statue. Once the primary subject had been identified, however, the painting takes on new historical and political valence.[16] George Gage came from an ancient Catholic family in England and became an international entrepreneur, mixing art connoisseurship with actual political diplomacy in the service of the Roman Church or its secular affiliates. He had converged in

Rome with the earl of Arundel, Inigo Jones, and Tobie Mathew, all at that time English Catholics, and was in 1614 there ordained a Jesuit priest by Cardinal Bellarmine. He became an intimate of Rubens, and as such was a magnet for Prince Charles when in October 1620 he visited England, exciting the heir to the throne with ideas of possessing European masterpieces. Whether painted in London in 1620 or in Venice in 1622, the portrait carries considerable political significance. Beginning in May 1621, Gage embarked on what Howarth has called "a strenuous period of shuttle diplomacy,"[17] traveling between London, Madrid, and Rome carrying secret messages, especially regarding the negotiations for Charles's marriage to the Spanish Infanta. In a long letter to Sir Henry Goodyer, dated September 19, 1622, John Donne described the fall of the Palatinate, James I's notorious "Directions" to preachers to avoid topical matters, and added: "Mr. Gage is returning to Rome, but of his Negotiation I dare say nothing by a Letter of adventure."[18] At that time the papacy, in the context of the Spanish Marriage negotiations, was already inspired by the hopes of England's reconversion, and Gage's negotiations were seen by Gregory XV as a means to that end.[19]

Van Dyck's portrait of Gage, moreover, identifies him as a Jesuit, or so we can deduce by comparing it with his portrait of Virginio Cesarini, painted in 1623 in Cesarini's final illness (Fig. 6). As David Freedberg has explained, Cesarini, the editor and defender of Galileo against the Catholic Church, nevertheless grew closer to the Jesuits in Rome as his illness progressed and expressed a wish to be buried in Jesuit habit.[20] Van Dyck's visual memorial to him fulfills that request. If we compare it with the portrait of Gage, the similarity of garb is confirmed by the identical treatment of the hands, each with a ring on the left little finger. Gage apparently carried on his sacral role along with his entrepreneurial ones. When the Treasurer, Lord Weston, died in March 1634, George Garrard reported to Strafford in Ireland:

> It is whispered and believed that he died a Roman Catholic, and had all the Ceremonies of that Church performed to him at his death. And none but such were present with him when he died, . . . Moore, Gifford, Winston, *Gage*, Watson, and some others of his Family.[21]

The portrait of Gage was therefore one of the earliest of the *English* portraits by Van Dyck that spoke to the existence of what one might call a Catholic politics of the portrait. It also spoke to the Arundel connection. Thomas Howard, second earl of Arundel, had met Gage in Rome in the winter of 1613–14. Dudley Carleton reported Gage to have been in "much resort" with him at that time, a connection that, since it was based partly on art acquisition, was surely continued; and, considering that a "ritratto de Mr Gage" was recorded in Arundel's collection, it is conceivable that this was the Van Dyck itself. It is therefore probably connected, as a product of this first English sojourn by Van Dyck, to his first portrait of Arundel himself, painted very late in 1620 or early 1621, and recently the subject of a monograph by Christopher White.[22]

I promised that we would return to Arundel, who would become one of Van Dyck's most important patrons, and whose extraordinary collection of art at one point contained the original Holbein group portrait of the More family. It also contained the Holbein portraits of Henry Howard, Earl of Surrey, executed for treason by Henry VIII in 1547, and of Surrey's father, Thomas Howard, third duke of Norfolk. Both portraits were in fact featured in a strange late group portrait of the Arundel family by Philip Fruytiers (Fig. 7), which is supposed to be based on a Van Dyck watercolor, and which also features the armor worn by the second duke of Norfolk at Flodden Field. Christopher White sees behind this somewhat unfortunate image an intention to echo the Holbein portrait of the More family, but it even more clearly echoes the 1590 adaptation for the family of Thomas More II, with its portrait of Anne Cresacre on the wall behind the family.

White's central argument is that Arundel grew up with an overriding ambition to reestablish the Howard family's titles, possessions, and standing, "which should by right have placed him second only to royalty in both status and wealth."[23] To do this, however, meant passing over, at least iconographically, an inconvenient section of the family history. Arundel's father, Philip Howard, the first earl, died in the Tower in 1595 as a Catholic, having been converted by the performance of Edmund Campion in the debates with Protestant theologians in the Tower, debates which were promptly printed. His wife, Anne Dacres, had sheltered Robert Southwell, among other priests, in one of the family's houses and permitted the operation of an illicit press therein. This press may have produced Southwell's *Epistle of Comfort*, originally a personal letter to Arundel in the Tower.[24] After Southwell's execution the countess possessed "a relic, one of the bones of his feet and wore it constantly, exerting herself in every possible way to follow his edicts."[25] It seems virtually impossible that the second earl, having been brought up by this woman who later came to live with him, would not have retained a deeper Catholic strain under his conformity, which was expressed at Christmas 1616 by his taking communion in King James's chapel.[26] In 1613–14, however, he had caused a scandal by visiting, while still a Catholic, the Holy City. English travelers were expressly forbidden to visit Rome.[27] Certainly his wife Aletheia was a strong Catholic, shown here in Daniel Mytens's portrait of her (Fig. 8) wearing not one but two crosses round her neck. While their two eldest sons were educated as Protestants, their fifth son, William Howard, later Viscount Stafford, was brought up as Catholic, and would be executed in 1680 for complicity in the Popish Plot. Their grandson Philip, who went with his grandfather and siblings to Europe when the civil war broke out, became a Dominican in 1645, admittedly over his grandfather's bitter objections. Later he became a cardinal.

When Van Dyck returned to England in 1632, other Arundel portraits would follow—family and dynastic portraits: of Arundel with his grandson Thomas; of Lord Maltravers, the second son who became the heir; and of William Howard, the youngest son. In view of the scandal created when Maltravers secretly married, in 1626, Lady Elizabeth Stuart against King Charles's wishes, a piece of dynastic disruption for which Arundel himself was first imprisoned and long kept out favor, the portrait implies at least reinstatement. We will return to other possible meanings later. More obviously symbolic was the group portrait of Arundel with Aletheia in the "Madagascar" portrait (Fig. 9), from which the central figures were later, after the family was effectively disbanded, transferred to the Fruytiers family piece, which attempts to restore unity under the auspices of an ancient ancestry. Here significance of the huge globe, with its discredited colonialist project attached to it, along with a monarchical nuance that might well have been seen as over-reaching, has been transferred to the sixteenth-century pageant shield that, legend once had it, derived from the earl of Surrey.[28] Given the importance of Arundel's collections, and the ideological defense of them published in 1638 by

Arundel's librarian, Franciscus Junius,[29] images of Arundel and his family would inevitably be linked thematically to the status and function of the visual arts in Caroline England. The question then becomes: what message would these portraits convey?

In his remarkable pro-Catholic study, *Charles I and the Court of Rome*, Gordon Albion documents the Catholic Spring of the late 1630s (the term is mine, not Albion's, and it alludes, of course to the Prague Spring of 1968) when the community at court blossomed under the influence of the papal agent to England, George Conn. According to Albion (although David Mathew was more cautious)[30] there was definitely a climate change in their favor. Charles himself apparently liked Conn immensely, not least because Conn was an educated and cultured Scot who could talk endlessly about art. He had also, not incidentally, written a book defending the reputation of the king's grandmother, Mary, Queen of Scots. Having worked as Cardinal Barberini's secretary, he came to England warmly recommended by Walter Montagu, with a mandate to support the queen, but he talked endlessly with the king, to the great dissatisfaction of the Puritan privy councilors. When challenged about his intimacy with Charles, Conn would reply that the king's "interest in pictures and sculpture was known to all, and, if his Majesty and he chose to discuss the arts in public, it was that all might hear."[31] We now know, or think we know, that Charles was as subtle as Conn. Charles was never, it seems, tempted to do more than indulge his wife and his own tastes, and the hopes of Pope Urban and of Cardinal Barberini for a reunification of England with Rome as the end result of the royal marriage were seriously deluded. But in the course of detailing the rise of Catholic optimism, Albion gives evidence, taken from Conn's correspondence with his superiors, of the role of the Arundels in this changed environment. In 1635 Arundel had a conversation with Panzani about what it would take to persuade Charles to grant the Catholics liberty of conscience, adding that he himself would be willing to go as Ambassador to Rome (p. 172).[32] Lady Aletheia was one of Conn's most fervent supporters; and in 1638, Peter Fytton, Roman agent to the English clergy, was amazed to be taken by Arundel himself to kiss the king's hand, while the countess declared that before Conn's arrival "she would not have dared to invite a priest to her table for a million pounds" (p. 165).

At any rate, both Arundel and his countess would appear in Hans Vanderpill's vast political caricature, *Magna Britannia Divisa* (Fig. 10). As Erica Veevers has demonstrated, this satirical print, published in 1642, creates a "Processio Romana" in which appear, numbered and with keys to their identity, all the figures to whom were attributed the religious dissentions in England that led to the civil war.[33] George Conn appears therein as Father O'Cony, Number 4 in the procession, as befitted his warming-up role in the Catholic Spring. And much later in the procession there appear the not-quite-identified figures of "The English Italianated lady, Dimittite nobis debita nostra," and "the great E[arl] her husband. Propter antiquam nostram rem."

Also featured in this hostile line-up was Endymion Porter, whose agency in expanding the king's art collections had begun with the acquisition of the Mantua paintings, and who had been a trusted servant of Charles since the Spanish Marriage negotiations in which Porter had played a considerable though unsuccessful role. Porter, whose role as courtier required his attendance on Charles at church, was forced to keep his Catholic sympathies secret, a problem discussed in the correspondence between Conn and Cardinal Barberini,[34] but he had married a woman who was, according to Erica Veevers, "an ardent Catholic and the busiest proselytiser at court."[35] Olivia Porter, one of the first converts to Catholicism in Henrietta Maria's circle, was herself painted by Van Dyck c. 1637.[36] One of the earliest portraits Van Dyck had produced on his return to England was a family group of Endymion and Olive with three of their children.[37] But in 1635 or thereabouts Van Dyck took the remarkable step of pairing himself with Endymion Porter in what we might describe as "Self-Portrait with close friend," a wonderful picture now in the Prado (Fig. 11). This is the only Van Dyck self-portrait with a friend to share the canvas; the oval format is particularly intimate; and as the painter's left hand almost touches Porter's, Van Dyck points to his breast with the index finger of the right, seemingly to indicate emotion.

Another subject of Van Dyck's was Sir Kenelm Digby, who had converted away from Catholicism in 1630, and converted back in 1635, announcing his change of heart to Archbishop Laud and Sir John Coke.[38] He must have imagined that Laud would not be entirely horrified. Digby's tiny portrait also appeared in *Magna Britannia Divisa*, along with that of the royalist poet Sir John Suckling, whom Van Dyck had painted in clothes sumptuous to the point, one would think, of immobility, and holding an open folio edition of Shakespeare. Suckling too converted to Catholicism. Inigo Jones, another overt Catholic whose portrait, one of three by Van Dyck, was later engraved for the famous *Icones,* does not himself appear in Vanderpill's broadside, but the entire structure, visual and verbal, is a parody of the masques for which Jones was famous. *Magna Divisa Britannia* therefore constitutes independent though hostile testimony that these men were seen as *connected,* as part of a long trailing Catholic community with Conn near the beginning, the queen at its center, and the war as the sting in its tail.

Of course there were dozens of figures identified in this broadside who did not sit to Van Dyck, most of them Catholic clerics. Oliver Millar, who rightly observed that not all of Van Dyck's patrons were courtiers, nor did they all become royalists during the civil war, added that some of the finest portraits were done for or of "such powerful and Puritan figures" as Robert Rich, Earl of Warwick, Francis Russell, Earl of Bedford, Elizabeth Howard, Countess of Peterborough, and Philip Lord Wharton.[39] This observation introduces the question of religion only indirectly, but clearly with the intent to absolve Van Dyck of being a partisan painter. Once the question of religion has been raised, however, it is startling to discover how many of Van Dyck's sitters, especially the women, were either members of old Catholic families, were known to have recently converted, or converted some time after their portraits were painted.

Much of this evidence has been accumulated by Malcolm Rogers, in a brilliant article on Van Dyck's portrait of George Stuart, Seigneur d'Aubigny.[40] Lord George, along with his two brothers Lord John and Lord Bernard (also the subject of a double portrait by Van Dyck) (Fig. 12) had been raised as Catholics. In 1638 Lord George secretly married Lady Katherine Howard, daughter of the second earl of Suffolk, who promptly took on her new husband's religion. This was one of the scandals of conversion that George Garrard, the old friend of John Donne, reported to Strafford in Ireland. In May 1638 Garrard wrote to Strafford that "our great Women fall away every day. My Lady Maltravers is declared a Papist; and also my Lady Katherine Howard, but tis Love hath been the principal Agent in her conversion."[41] Rogers decoded the portrait of Lord George Stuart, with its motto "Me

fermior Amor" carved on a rock, as an allusion both to this marriage and to the displeasure it caused the king. Lady Maltravers,
Lady Katherine Howard's fellow convert in 1638, was Lord George
Stuart's sister, Elizabeth, who had also married against the king's
wishes. In 1626 she married Arundel's eldest surviving son, a
match for which his father had been briefly sent to the Tower.
Her portrait by Van Dyck was inscribed on the back by Elizabeth
herself in 1649, leaving it to her husband and his heirs. Significantly, the bequest is written under the sign of a cross. A second inscription dates the portrait as "drawne by Sr. Antony van-
dike In 1635."[42]

It is worth returning to Garrard's letter to Strafford, however, to
get the full flavor of this event and its connection to the arts. On
May 10, 1638, the year in which the Scots pledged the Covenant
in February and Charles signed with them the humiliating Treaty
of Berwick, Garrard wrote to Strafford describing a recent procession by the Spanish Ambassador, including Irishmen with beads
about their necks. "'Tis true," he wrote:

> notwithstanding all the Care and Vigilancy the King and Pre-
> lates take for the suppressing of Popery, yet it much increaseth
> about London, and these pompous Shews of the Sepulchre con-
> tribute much to it, for they grow common; they are not only set
> up now in the Queen's Chapel, for which there is some Reason,
> but also in the Ambassadors Houses, in Con's Lodgings, nay
> at York-House, and in my Lord of Worcester's House, if they be
> not Lyars who tell it. Our great Women fall away every Day. My
> Lady Maltravers is declared a Papist; and also my Lady Katherine
> Howard, but 'tis Love hath been the principal Agent in her Con-
> version. (2:165)

In using the phrase "the principal Agent," Garrard was punning on
the role that the Papal Agent Conn was assumed to have played at
court, here upstaged by Eros. Garrard was much more impressed
with the growth of the Catholic community at court than was, as
I have mentioned, the modern historian David Mathew, and he
made a strong inferential connection between "pompous Shews"
and conversions to or consolidations of the Catholic community.
Earlier, on January 8, 1635, he had reported to Strafford a major
event in the art world of the time:

This last Month the Queen's Chapel in Somerset-House-Yard was consecrated by her Bishop; the ceremonies lasted three Days, Massing, Preaching, and Singing of Litanies, and such a glorious Scene built over their Altar, the Glory of Heaven, Inigo Jones never presented a more curious Piece in any of the Masks at Whitehall; with this our English ignorant Papists are mightily taken. I went to see it one evening; much or more flocking of English Papists is to this Chapel now, than heretofore, which I am sorry to know. (1:505)

Inigo Jones, himself a Catholic, was the architect of the new chapel building; and Garrard's intuitive connection between this building and his masques has been confirmed by Veevers, who has shown that the masque *The Temple of Love*, presented in 1635, was advance promotion for the chapel itself.[43] But the "glorious Scene" Garrard refers to was not created by Jones, but rather by François Dieussart, a Flemish sculptor brought over by the Capuchins to celebrate the establishment in the Chapel of their Arch-Confraternity. It is surely no coincidence that Arundel seems also to have been an agent in Dieussart's coming to England, and that Arundel commissioned several busts from the sculptor for his own collection, including one of himself and one of Charles I, signed and dated 1636.[44] But to return to the chapel: behind the altar, as Father Cyprien described the temporary "scene" or stage setting, a Paraclete appeared over seven ranges of clouds filled with angels, the whole "painted and placed according to the rules of perspective" so that the illusion was immeasurably grander than the reality. Circles of decreasing size led the eye to the Sacrament at the center of the design, which was glowing with gold and lighted by over four hundred lights.[45]

Later, probably in 1638, which seems to have been an exceptionally busy year for Van Dyck, he painted a double portrait of Katherine Howard, now Lady Aubigny, and her sister-in-law, Frances Stuart, Countess of Portland. Rogers infers from the extreme emphasis in this portrait on pearls, associated with both St. Margaret of Antioch and the Virgin Mary herself, that it celebrates the pregnancy of both women, who each gave birth early in 1639.[46] Frances Stuart, who married Jerome, the eldest son of the crypto-Catholic Treasurer Weston, was one of the queen's attendants identified by Veevers as herself of Catholic persuasion. The Jesuit priest

Henry Hawkins, who dedicated the various volumes of Nicholas Caussin's *The Holy Court* to Henrietta Maria and her ladies, made Frances Weston the sponsor of Volume 3.[47] And Treasurer Weston himself, always suspected (correctly) of being a crypto-Catholic, was another of Van Dyck's subjects.

In 1637 Van Dyck painted Lady Dorothy Savage, Viscountess Andover, who converted to Roman Catholicism at the time of her marriage, in a double portrait with her sister Elisabeth, Lady Thimbleby (Fig. 13). Rogers remarks on the controversy caused by this conversion and gives pictorial evidence that this fanciful portrait was painted at the time of the wedding. Lady Andover wears the saffron robes of a Roman bride, and her sister "adopts the veil and attitude of *Pudicitia*" (p. 264). An angel with a basket of roses, the attribute of St. Dorothea of Cappadocia, attends the bride. Even more directly than in the case of Lady Katherine Howard and Lord George Stuart, then, the portrait might be considered as celebrating the conversion as well as the marriage. Van Dyck also painted Anne Boteler, Countess of Newport, the sister of Olivia Porter, who converted to Catholicism in 1637, causing another major scandal reported to Strafford by Garrard.[48]

Another interesting cluster of persons were the actual or implied subject of a group portrait that has recently received much critical attention. In 1638 Van Dyck painted the dramatist Thomas Killigrew[49] with William, Lord Crofts, evidently participating in an act of mourning (Fig. 14). Graham Parry[50] and Malcolm Rogers have both deciphered the portrait as referring to the deaths of the two sisters of Lord Crofts, Cecilia, who had married Killigrew, and Anne, who had married Thomas, Lord Wentworth, Earl of Cleveland. Both young women died in early 1638. On October 9, 1637, Garrard had reported to Strafford that "Mr. Will Crofts is fled into Italy, being lately reconciled to the Church of Rome" (2:115). On July 3, 1638, he reported that Crofts has returned to England but "not yet admitted to the Court" (2:181); the memorial painting, perhaps, performs that gesture of acceptance by way of pity. Crofts sits watching his friend Killigrew, holding and pointing towards a blank sheet of paper, a symbol, according to Rogers, of "the absoluteness of the loss" (p. 265). Killigrew has a matching sheet of paper, which he barely still holds in flaccid fingers, but which dimly shows a drawing of two female statues on pedestals, presumably a design for the monument to be erected to the dead sisters. Neither

Rogers nor Parry, however, assigns any significance to a detail which may indicate either that Killigrew too was a convert (unlikely, given his reputation for scurrility) or that his dead wife had been: a crucifix attached to his right sleeve, displaying Cecilia's initials. As with the crosses mentioned earlier in this essay, this was not an ornament likely to be flaunted by conforming Protestants. In December 1635 Garrard had reported to Strafford that Walter Montagu, another notorious convert, "triumphs in his new Religion at Paris; . . . he wears a Chain of Beads with a Cross hanging at them about his Neck, waits on that King whensoever he goes to Mass, writes over to his Friends here, that he is not only reconciled to the Church of Rome, but he is ready to die a Martyr for his Religion" (1:490). "Oh vain Man!" concluded Garrard, referring simultaneously to the religious instability and the ostentatious display of Catholic symbols.[51]

I have, obviously, ignored the well-traveled field of Van Dyck's portraits of the royal family themselves. But it should not be forgotten that Henrietta Maria was several times portrayed by Van Dyck wearing a crucifix. One of his most important commissions, moreover, was the "Charles I in three positions," which was sent to Rome as a model for Bernini to make a bust of the king. David Howarth has pointed out that, however fantastic it may now seem, Urban VIII granted Henrietta Maria the privilege of access to Bernini in the hope that this extraordinary favor, combined with the impact of the bust when completed, would actually facilitate England's return to Catholicism. As Cardinal Barberini wrote to Cardinal Mazarin:

> The statues go on prosperously nor shall I hesitate to rob Rome of her most valuable ornaments, if in exchange we might be so happy as to have the King of England's name among those princes who submit to the Apostolic See.[52]

Howarth did not, however, draw the conclusion to which this essay is tending, that Van Dyck himself was a knowing instrument in this plan, and that there was a politics—a strategic politics driven by religion—to the portraits of his English period. Whereas those of his Dutch and Roman residences were usually and straightforwardly of Catholic subjects, and emerged side by side with Counter-Reformation religious paintings, those of his English period created instead—for the brief spring of seven years' duration—the image of a court in which Roman Catholics were gorgeously and confidently omnipresent. Double portraits and family portraits were themselves, perhaps, a part of the message. The emphasis on children and pregnancy—a basis of encomium always for Henrietta Maria herself—also implied the increase of their numbers; and the result was a cumulative portrait of a particular Catholic community on the rise, not an intimidated and penalized minority.

Figure 1.   The Executions of Thomas More and John Fisher, from Richard Verstegan, *Theatrum Crudelitatum Haereticorum* (Antwerp, 1587, 1597). Beinecke Rare Book and Manuscript Library, Yale University

Figure 2. The Execution of Mary Queen of Scots, from Richard Verstegan, *Theatrum Crudelitatum Haereticorum* (Antwerp, 1587, 1597). Beinecke Rare Book and Manuscript Library, Yale University

FAMILIA THOMÆ MORI ANGL: CANCELL:

Thomas Morus. Æt:50. Alicia Thomæ Mori uxor Æt:57. Iohannes Morus pater Æt:76. Iohannes Morus Thomæ filius Æt:9. Anna Grisacria Iohannis Mori Sponsa Æt:15 Margareta Ropera Thomæ Mori filia Æt:. Elisabeta Dauncia Thomæ Mori filia Æt:. Cæcilia Hereina Thomæ Mori filia Æt:20 Margareta Gigs Clementis uxor Mori filiabus Condiscipula et cognata Æt:22 Henricus Patensonus Thomæ Mori morio Æt:40.

Figure 3. Hans Holbein the Younger, *Sir Thomas More and His Family*, 1527–28. Öffentliche Kunstsammlung, Kupferstichkabinett Basel (photocredit Martin Bühler)

Figure 4.   Rowland Lockey after Hans Holbein, *Sir Thomas More, His Father, His Household, and His Descendants*, 1593. By courtesy of National Portrait Gallery, London

Figure 5.   Anthony Van Dyck, *George Gage and Companions*, 1620–22.
By courtesy of National Gallery, London

Figure 6.   Anthony Van Dyck, *Virginio Cesarini*, 1623.
The Hermitage, St. Petersburg

Figure 7.   Philip Fruytiers, *Thomas Howard, 14th Earl of Arundel and His Countess with Their Grandchildren and a Dwarf.*
Reproduced by the kind permission of His Grace the Duke of Norfolk

Figure 8.   Daniel Mytens, *Aletheia, Countess of Arundel and Surrey,*
         ca. 1618. By courtesy of National Portrait Gallery, London

Figure 9. Anthony Van Dyck, *The Madagascar Portrait*. Reproduced by the kind permission of His Grace the Duke of Norfolk

Figure 10.   *Divisa Magna Britannia* (1642). By permission of The British Library

Figure 11.   Anthony Van Dyck, *Self-portrait with Endymion Porter*, ca. 1635.
The Prado, Madrid

Figure 12.   Anthony Van Dyck, *Lord John Stuart and His Brother,*
Lord Bernard Stuart, ca. 1638. By courtesy of National Gallery, London

Figure 13.   Anthony Van Dyck, *Lady Dorothy Savage, Viscountess of Andover, with her sister, Elizabeth, Lady Thimbleby.* By courtesy of National Gallery, London

Figure 14.   Anthony Van Dyck, *Thomas Killigrew and William, Lord Crofts.*
The Royal Collection © 2000, Her Majesty Queen Elizabeth II

NOTES

1. John Bossy, *The English Catholic Community 1570–1850* (Oxford, 1976), 1.

2. See David Mathew, *Catholicism in England. The Portrait of a Minority: Its Culture and Tradition* (London, 1936, 1948).

3. Eamon Duffy, *The Stripping of the Altars: Traditional Religion in England c 1400–c.1580* (New Haven and London, 1992).

4. Arthur Marotti, "Southwell's Remains: Catholicism and Anti-Catholicism in Early Modern England," in *Texts and Cultural Change in Early Modern England* (London, 1997), 37.

5. Despite the excellent edition produced by James McDonald, self-identified as "Priest of the Congregation of the Holy Cross," and Nancy Pollard Brown, *The Poems of Robert Southwell, SJ.* (Oxford, 1967). Typically, they were preceded by another Catholic editor, Father James H. McDonald, who identified the scattered works of Southwell in his *Poems and Prose Writings of Robert Southwell, S.J.: A Bibliographical Study* (Oxford, 1937).

6. For instance, the collection of essays celebrating the first centenary of Campion Hall, Oxford, *The Reckoned Expense: Edmund Campion and the Early English Jesuits,* ed. Thomas M. McCoog (Woodbridge, U.K., 1996). See also Peter Lake, "Anti-Popery: The Structure of a Prejudice," in *Conflict in Early Stuart England: Studies in Religion and Politics 1603–1643,* ed. Richard Cust and Ann Hughes (London and New York, 1989), 72–106; and Alison Shell, "Catholic Texts and Anti-Catholic Prejudice in the 17th-century Book Trade," in *Censorship and the Control of Print in England and France, 1600–1900,* ed. Robin Myers and Michael Harris (Winchester, 1992).

7. Marotti, "Southwell's Remains," 62, n. 37. He also observes that these frescoes were reproduced in a printed text, *Ecclesiae Anglicanae Trophaea,* published in Rome in 1589.

8. Richard Verstegan, *Theatrum Crudelitatum haereticorum nostri temporis* (Antwerp, 1587, 1597).

9. Clark Hulse, "Dead Man's Treasure: The Cult of Thomas More," in *The Production of Renaissance Culture,* ed. David Lee Miller, Sharon O'Dair, and Harold Weber (Ithaca, New York, and London, 1994), 208–209, n. 16; Hulse is citing Stanley Morison, *The Likeness of Sir Thomas More: An Iconographical Survey of Three Centuries* (New York, 1963), 21, and John Rowlands, *The Paintings of Hans Holbein the Younger* (Oxford, 1985), 71.

10. Hulse cites Stanley Morison's account of the composition as "an example of . . . adaptation of a religious formula to a secular purpose. . . . In the 'Darmstadt Madonna,' which he painted in 1526, the Meyer family

are grouped round, and radiate from, the Madonna and Child in the top centre: if there were a similar nucleus in the empty foreground of the More family group, it would become an Adoration." See Morison, *The Likeness of Thomas More: An Iconographical Survey of Three Centuries* (New York, 1963), 21. The phrase "empty foreground," however, is misleading.

11. In the first copy made by Rowland Lockey More and his clock have been placed dramatically on the central axis, with the clock's weights hanging symbolically over his head.

12. Lorne Campbell, *Renaissance Portraits* (New Haven and London, 1990), 209; citing William Camden's *History of . . . Elizabeth* (London, 1688), 340; and W. K. Boyd, *Calendar of State Papers Relating to Scotland and Mary, Queen of Scots,* vol. 8 (London, 1914), 687.

13. John Donne, *Pseudo-Martyr,* ed. Anthony Raspa (Montreal and Kingston, 1993), "An Advertisement to the Reader."

14. Dennis Flynn, *John Donne and the Ancient Catholic Nobility* (Bloomington and Indianapolis, 1995), 22.

15. See David Howarth, *Images of Rule: Art and Politics in the English Renaissance, 1485–1649* (Berkeley and Los Angeles, 1997), 270. Howarth cites a letter to Charles from his Italian banker Filippo Burlamachi, probably dated 17 October, complaining about his inability to finance *both* the Mantua purchase *and* the British expedition to relieve La Rochelle.

16. The identification was made by Oliver Millar, "Notes on Three Pictures by Van Dyck," *Burlington Magazine* 111 (1969): 414–17.

17. Howarth, *Images of Rule,* 69. For Gage's career, see also Susan Barnes, "Van Dyck and George Gage," in *Art and Patronage in the Caroline Courts,* ed. David Howarth (Cambridge, 1993), 1–11.

18. Donne, *Letters to Severall Persons of Honour* (1651), ed. M. Thomas Hester (Delmar, N. Y., 1977), 231.

19. Howarth, *Images of Rule,* 67–69, cites a letter from Sir Isaac Wake at the court of Savoy in Turin, dated June 1623, recording Gage's discomfiture after "the great negotiation at Rome" in not being given diplomatic privileges: "here they would not let him passe as a publique Minister," requiring him to pay duty on the "presents," presumably pictures, he was bringing back to England:

> which accident did a little mortifye him, as being unwilling to owe unto a third person the justification of his quality which he did presume to have been of such eminencye that he might better have given than taken certificats.

20. David Freedberg, "Van Dyck and Virginio Cesarini: A Contribution to the Study of Van Dyck's Roman Sojourns," in *Van Dyck 350,* ed. Susan J. Barnes and Arthur K. Wheelock, Jr., National Gallery of Art (Washington, D.C., 1994), 153–74.

21. *The Earl of Strafford's Letters and Dispatches,* 2 vols. (London, 1739), 1:389.

22. Christopher White, *Anthony van Dyck: Thomas Howard The Earl of Arundel* (Malibu, Calif., 1995). Because so much attention is there given to this early portrait of Arundel alone, it is neither discussed nor reproduced here.

23. White, *Anthony van Dyck: Thomas Howard The Earl of Arundel,* 3.

24. See McDonald and Pollard Brown, *The Poems of Robert Southwell,* xxvi–xxvii.

25. See Nancy Pollard Brown, "Robert Southwell: The Mission of the Written Word," in *The Reckoned Expense: Edmund Campion and the Early English Jesuits,* ed. Thomas M. McCoog, (Woodbridge, U.K., and Rochester, N.Y., 1996), 212.

26. The question of Arundel's sincerity in conforming, or rather of the real nature of his religious beliefs, is obviously impossible now of solution. Arundel's biographer Mary Hervey restated Clarendon's assessment that he was "thought not to be much concerned for religion" in more generous terms, while strenuously resisting the implication that Arundel's change of creed was prudential, a necessary move in his campaign to reinstate his family in its former dignities. "Against Roman Catholicism in its purely religious aspect, he had no quarrel. . . . Theological controversy was foreign to his bent of mind. Given the great truths on which all the religions profess to be founded, minor divergencies of doctrine seem to have left him cold." See Hervey, *The Life, Correspondence & Collections of Thomas Howard, Earl of Arundel* (Cambridge, 1921), 117. Hervey notes that the well-documented communion at Christmas 1616 *followed* Arundel's being invited into the Privy Council, from which Catholics were barred, rather than preceding it. This does not, however, preclude the possibility that James and Arundel negotiated the latter's official act of conformation as a condition of inclusion in the circles of power.

27. See Hervey, *Life,* 83–84, 89; and David Howarth, *Lord Arundel and His Circle* (New Haven and London, 1985), 51, who states that Arundel was questioned by the archbishop of Canterbury upon his return about the reasons for his Rome visit.

28. See *Patronage and Collecting in the Seventeenth Century: Thomas Howard, Earl of Arundel* (Ashmolean Museum Exhibition Catalogue, Oxford), 25. By the mid-eighteenth century it had acquired a fictional history recorded by George Vertue, that it had been given to Surrey by the Grand Duke of Tuscany at a tournament.

29. See Franciscus Junius, *The Painting of the Ancients* (London, 1638), 79–81: "Teastie and ambitiously severe censurers also have but small reason to finde fault with such great and wealthy men as with an excessive cost do buy for strife all manner of Art, valuing the rare works of great

Masters according to the delight & contentment that they find in them. Neither is it unlikely that brave and generous men sometimes resolve of their own accord to raise the price of pictures and statues, because they could not endure that such honest and innoxious delights should be generally condemned and contemned. . . . [Therefore] men of ordinary estates need not spend themselves that way . . . since great and generous spirits, furnish their houses with such things not onely for their private contemplation, but also for the free use of such as doe professe themselves to be Lovers and well-willers of Art, thinking their cost well bestowed when many doe daily resort to their galleries."

30. See Mathew, *Catholicism in England,* 78–80.

31. Gordon Albion, *Charles I and the Court of Rome: A Study in 17th Century Diplomacy* (London, 1935), 243. See also his account of how Charles delayed a Garter ceremony in order to show Conn his picture gallery (pp. 236–37).

32. Albion notes that this offer was not, perhaps, entirely altruistic, since an authorized visit to Rome would offer a great opportunity for connoisseurship.

33. See Erica Veevers, *Images of Love and Religion: Queen Henrietta Maria and Court Entertainments* (Cambridge, 1989), 207.

34. Albion, *Charles I and the Court of Rome,* 210.

35. Veevers, *Images of Love and Religion,* 86. Veevers has identified those members of Henrietta Maria's court who were either themselves Catholics or connected via patronage or family to members of that religion.

36. See Oliver Millar, *Van Dyck in England* (London, 1983), 78–79.

37. Ibid., no. 49, dates the portrait by way of the apparent age of the youngest child Philip, who had been born in 1628.

38. See R.T. Petersson, *Sir Kenelm Digby: The Ornament of England 1603–1665* (Cambridge, Mass., 1956), 95, 110, citing H.M.C. 12th Report (Melbourne Hall Papers), 2:64–65, and Laud, *Works,* 6:447–55, which contains his letter of reply. On August 14, 1636, Van Dyck wrote to Franciscus Junius, whose *Painting of the Ancients* he had evidently seen in manuscript, congratulating him on the work and requesting a motto which could be placed on the version of his portrait of Digby intended for the *Icones.* The face of Junius himself was similarly honored. See Millar, *Van Dyck in England,* no. 64, p. 103.

39. Ibid., p. 32.

40. Malcolm Rogers, "Van Dyck's Portrait of *Lord George Stuart, Seigneur d'Aubigny,* and Some Related Works," in *Van Dyck 350,* ed. Susan J. Barnes and Arthur K. Wheelock, National Gallery of Art (Washington, D.C., 1994), 263–79.

41. *The Earl of Strafford's Letters and Dispatches,* 2 vols. (London, 1739), 2:165.

42. Millar, *Van Dyck in England*, no. 19.

43. Veevers, *Images of Love and Religion*, 136–41.

44. See *Patronage and Collecting*, 12.

45. Veevers, *Images of Love and Religion*, 165–67. She found this description in Thomas Birch, *The Court and Times of Charles the First*, ed. Robert Folkestone Williams, 2 vols. (London, 1848), 2:311–13.

46. Rogers, "Van Dyck's Portrait," 274–75.

47. Veevers, *Images of Love and Religion*, 79.

48. Strafford, *Letters and Dispatches*, 2:128–29. What Garrard wrote, on November 9, 1637, was extremely informative: "Here hath been an horrible Noise about the Lady Newport's become a Roman Catholic." Newport complained to Laud "of those whom he thought had been Instruments in the conversion of his Wife, naming Seignior Con, Wat Mountague, and Sir Toby Matthew." But, continued Garrard, "the Truth is, neither Wat Mountague, nor Toby Matthew, had any hand in this Particular; my lady Dutchess of Buckingham [Katherine Manners], her sister Porter, and Seignior Con, have been chief Agents in her Conversion, though it is whooly laid upon the Capuchins, and the Queen hath since sent for their Rector, hath chid him, and admonished him from doing the like again, *especially to Women of Quality*" (emphasis added).

49. This was one of several portraits of Killigrew and his family. In 1638 Van Dyck also painted a full-length portrait of Killigrew by himself (Millar, *Van Dyck in England*, no. 39), of Anne Kirk, Killigrew's sister and one of the queen's dressers (ibid., no. 35), and of Sir William Killigrew, Thomas's elder brother (ibid., no. 38).

50. Graham Parry, "Van Dyck and the Caroline Court Poets," in *Van Dyck 350*, ed. Susan J. Barnes and Arthur K. Wheelock, National Gallery of Art (Washington, D.C., 1994), 253.

51. When Van Dyck married the Catholic Mary Ruthven in 1640, he painted her holding a loose bracelet of dark pearls with a crucifix. See Rogers, "Van Dyck's Portrait," 375–76.

52. Howarth, *Images of Rule*, 147.

CHAPTER FIVE

Cartography and Community in the Hispanic World

Richard L. Kagan

Writing in 1531, the famous Spanish humanist, Juan Luis Vives, examined the relationship between observation and knowledge. "Observation," he wrote, "begins with the eye." Vives then distinguished between seeing—a sensory phenomenon—and understanding or judgment which, as part of philosophy, properly belonged to the mind.[1]

Vives' distinction between seeing and knowing harks back to Aristotle's *De Anima*, but the Spaniard was one of the first thinkers to apply this particular concept to the study of paintings and maps. According to Vives, the "description" of "a man, a tree, either singly or in groups, just as a house, a city, a region, a town . . . belongs to the realm of the senses, and it is not very difficult, since it is relatively easy to paint what is in front of one's eyes." In contrast, Vives noted that it was "far more difficult to paint things that do not belong to the realm of the senses," a category which embraced the "essence" of things together with more abstract matters such as the nature of God.[2]

As most budding artists would readily attest, Vives' argument about the ease of painting what is in front of one's eyes is overstated, but his formulation of the difference between observation and understanding relates directly to the issue this essay would like to address, namely, city views that go beyond superficial description in an effort to capture not just the "look" of a town but, as Vives understood it, something of its "essence" as well. I will refer to views of the first sort as chorographic views, the latter as communicentric views.[3]

Chorographic views hardly require an introduction as they are the kind of city view we are readily familiar with, and today they can be readily found on the rack of picture postcards of cities worldwide. In early modern Europe, when these images first circulated in the form of woodcuts and engravings included in atlases and travel books, the names used to refer to this class of images varied widely, often in accordance with the angle of vision employed. Consequently, these images were variously known as profiles, prospects, portraits, bird's eye views, and ground plans; there were also plans with elevations, hypsographic views, ichnographic views, ichnoscenographic views, and so forth.[4] The lexicon is confusing, and still not totally sorted out. But whatever the precise nomenclature employed, such images simply described the "look" of a town, generally by mapping its built structure or urbs. In this respect, chorographic views approximate what Vives understood as seeing, mere observation or description. Yet as Vives understood it, seeing is one thing, knowledge another, and the gap between them is not easily bridged. With reference to towns, the former suggests a passing, somewhat superficial acquaintance, the latter a deeper understanding grounded in the town's history, the shared experiences of its inhabitants, etc. Put simply, the tourist "sees" a town, the resident "knows" it.

A similar gap separates the chorographic from the communicentric view. The former, customarily employing the artistic equivalent of a wide-angle lens, offers what one scholar has defined as a "distant overview" of a town.[5] In sixteenth-century Europe, the number of such views multiplied, offering, as in the case of the 1550 edition of Sebastian Münster's *Cosmographia*, dozens of conventional, if somewhat bloodless, descriptions of individual towns. To correct this deficiency, Georg Braun and Franz Hogenberg, editors of the *Civitates orbis terrarum* (1572–1618), encouraged their contributors to pepper their townscapes with folkloric elements and genre scenes. Such details, they wrote, would make "everything so clear that he [the viewer] seems to be seeing the actual town or place before his eyes."[6] Despite this boast, most chorographic views suffered from what Vives had defined as "mere observation," seeing without knowing. The result is that even those views which were topographically accurate did not—and indeed could not—enable a viewer to "know" a town, to penetrate its essence, a problem that the Spanish artist El Greco seemed intuitively to have understood in his *View and Plan of Toledo* (Fig. 1), c. 1610, when, within the confines of a single canvas, he offered a multivalent image of Toledo that included a ground plan, a perspective view, a model of an important building, and several allegorical images that referred to different aspects of the city's past— its antiquity in the guise of a river god; a cornucopia signaling the city's abundant agricultural resources; and its Christianity in the form of an emblem referring to the miracle of the Virgin Mary descending from heaven to present a chasuble to Ildefonsus, the sixth-century bishop of Toledo who had defended her virginity.[7] Compared with Van den Wyngaerde's 1563 view of the city, a topographically accurate chorographic view that portrayed Toledo as seen from the north, the *View and Plan* suggests that there was no single nor simple way of representing a city.[8] Indeed, El Greco's decision to incorporate these various ways of representing a city into a single image suggests that he understood that chorography, for all of its scientific pretensions, did not and indeed could not exhaust the "image" of the city. A perspective view and a ground plan helped orient a viewer, offering, if you will, an introduction to the city, but these images could never substitute, as Vives had suggested, for knowing what a city was like. For this, representations of a city's physical fabric, its *urbs*, would not suffice. Such knowledge also required intimate acquaintance with its history, legends, and traditions, that is, the human element in cities, and what I will refer to as *civitas*.

El Greco's *View and Plan of Toledo* speaks directly to the difference between chorographic and communicentric views. If the former focuses on urbs, the latter locks onto civitas, the human element in cities and one that, in an urban context, approximates what Vives described as the "essence of things." In this way the communicentric view is analogous to what the British geographer Peter Jackson calls a "map of meaning," which is a map of a particular locale that encodes certain clusters of beliefs, experiences, memories, and traditions—in other words, a sense of community— shared by the people who live there.[9] Scientific cartography, starting in the late fifteenth century, tended to reduce towns to a series of elemental forms and shapes, and subsequently represented them, either orthogonally or in perspective, in accordance with a mathematical grid. Vives defined this way of looking at a city as description, a term which, at least in the early modern period, also supposed a modicum of topographical accuracy and verisimilitude.

In contrast, the communicentric view, while it often incorporated some of the cartographic elements associated with description, generally did not pretend to offer a measured, topographically accurate representation of a particular town. Objectivity, in fact, was not its strong suit. Rather, it celebrated subjectivity, viewing the world, so to speak, through the lens of the community it purported to depict. The communicentric view tended, therefore, to be purposely idiosyncratic and filled with topographical distortions designed to enhance a town's size and overall importance. Another of its characteristics was its tendency to replace the "distant overviews" chorography preferred with close-up pictures that focus on particular structures—plazas, cathedrals, and other public monuments—that served as icons or symbols for the city as a whole. Not coincidentally, these structures were ones associated with the city's history and which also helped local inhabitants to forge a communal identity. Thus through what might be defined as the process of "metonymic representation," the communicentric projection singled out those locales that were integral to a particular community's definition of itself. In the case of Renaissance Rome this would probably have been St. Peter's basilica; in Venice, the cathedral of San Marco and its adjacent piazza, or in the case of Seville, the Giralda, the twelfth-century minaret which, transformed into the bell tower of the city's cathedral, became a symbol of the power and strength of the Catholic Church. Similarly, in the cities of Spanish America, artists tended to render cities "communicentrically" by focusing on the central plaza or square, the architectural element generally equated with the type of civilization that the Spaniards intended to impose on the New World.[10]

It follows that communicentric views were customarily fashioned for audiences quite different from the chorographic views published in atlases and travel books such as the *Civitates*. The latter tended to be the work of commercial publishers seeking an audience among readers lacking direct knowledge or experience with the cities that were represented. Publishers consequently favored panoramic views that emphasized a city's topographical situation together with its overall layout and design, a mode of representation which not only rendered faraway cities comprehensible to armchair travelers but offered these readers ready comparison with cities with which they were already familiar. In contrast, communicentric views were intended, in the first instance at least, for local audiences, presumably ones already well acquainted with the "look," that is, the physical appearance of the town being portrayed, as well as its customs, history, and traditions. The necessity, therefore, for description—the *sine qua non* of chorographic views—was of secondary importance. So too was the need to provide viewers a means of comparing one city with others. In fact, communicentric views did just the opposite, deliberately celebrating one city at the expense of others, much in the same way as Saul Steinberg's famous poster of Manhattan (1967) rendered that particular portion of New York City larger than life. Communicentric views had also embedded within them messages of special importance for the inhabitants of the community being portrayed, messages that could easily escape the untutored viewer who hailed from elsewhere. Communicentric views were in this sense unabashedly parochial as they self-consciously celebrated the particular virtues that helped to define individual towns.

Boosterism of this sort is, of course, nothing unusual; most urbanites tout the merits of their own community while deriding those of others. In the Hispanic world, however, communicentric views acquired special meanings inasmuch as town dwellers, starting in the Middle Ages, saw themselves perched somewhat perilously on the symbolic frontier separating and protecting Christianity from infidels, first in the guise of the Muslims they attempted to expel from the Iberian peninsula, later with the millions of *indios* they encountered in the New World. This particular vantage point transformed every town, no matter how humble, into a symbol of *policía*, a word that, starting in the eighteenth century, was generally equated with the forces of law and order but one that was previously interpreted, following Aristotle, in terms of the *res publica*, an organized community of citizens governed by law. *Policía* therefore became good government, especially the order, peace, and prosperity that sound government engendered. *Policía* was also skill, refinement, and manners, all closely tied to the Ciceronian term of *urbanitas*, a word whose meaning is best understood in opposition to *rusticitas*, or *rusticus*.[11] *Policía* thus represented a combination of two concepts: one public, linked to citizenship in an organized polity, the other connected to personal comportment and private life, both inseparable from urban life. In addition *policía* also contained an important religious component summarized in the term *"policía cristiana,"* a concept that was ultimately derived from Augustine as well as later Spanish writings about the "Christian commonwealth."[12] In fact, Christianity and the town were so closely connected in Spanish thought that most missionaries in the New World believed that it would be impossible to convert natives unless they were obliged to live in "organized towns" (*pueblos formados*).[13] Thus the policy, initiated in 1530s and designed to drag natives out of their traditional dwellings and into planned settlements called *reducciones*, was intended to hasten their conversion to what the Spaniards understood to be a civilized life.

Policía, in sum, implied all of the benefits that accrued from urban life: law, order, morality, and religion. *Policía*, moreover, lay at the very core of the empire that Spaniards sought to establish in the New World, an empire which, if examined from a purely jurisdictional perspective, was little more than an "empire of towns," each endowed, in theory at least, with *"buena policía."* Writers of the period evoked these connections in local histories and in various *laudatiae urbes*, a genre expressly devoted to urban self-aggrandizement and to the celebration of those virtues, both civic and religious, that rendered individual communities unique. The underlying idea in these works was to define the city less as a physical unit than as a moral or civic idea. Artists followed suit, although, as in the example of El Greco, they faced the additional challenge of combining the description of urbs and the evocation of civitas into a single visual frame. The solution to this particular problem was the communicentric view, that is, the view which "mapped" cities in ways that had little to do with description.

.   .   .

With respect to communicentric views in colonial Spanish America, I want to emphasize that the history of this class of image view in the Americas begins well before 1492. Natives throughout the Americas traditionally found various media—manuscripts, models, and maps—to express their own ideas about urban life, which can be illustrated by the "map" of Texúpa (Fig. 2), a small

Mixtec community in the highlands near Oaxaca, in south-central Mexico, dating from 1581.[14] This map belongs to the *Relaciones Geográficas*, Philip II's attempt to acquire detailed geographical information pertaining to his American realms. As part of this project, municipal officials were instructed to provide the monarch with a "description" or *traza*, that is, a ground plan of their town. In the case of Texúpa, the local artist, probably a native, did just this, as the ground plan inserted into the foreground of the map readily suggests. In this instance, however, the artist—like El Greco—depicted Texúpa communicentrically, notably through the use of several emblematic glyphs that referred to various chapters from the community's pre-Hispanic past, among them the pictogram—in this case a hill symbol in which the representation of a temple topped with a turquoise-blue jewel signified "place of blue," a reference to the community's older Mixtec name (Texúpa was a Nahuatl name imposed by the Aztecs at the end of the fifteenth century). Finally, it seems that the artist refers to the tensions accompanying the town's most recent conquest—by the Spaniards—by allowing footprints, the native symbol for movement and travel, to ride roughshod over Texúpa's new urban grid. In this sense, the glyphs inserted into the traza of Texúpa evoked memories of what native residents still thought of as the "place of blue."[15]

The Texúpa map is by no means unique—glyphs carrying similar historical messages appear in at least two dozen maps associated with the *Relaciones Geográficas*. Interpreted by art historians, these maps point to the survival of pre-Hispanic artistic traditions in the post-conquest era. They also suggest that indigenous notions of community had survived the Spanish conquest as well. Of central importance here is the idea that while a town might have certain distinguishing architectural features such as a temple or fortress, it was not primarily conceived of as a geographical or topographical unit, that is, as an urbs in the European sense of the term. A town was rather inseparable from the history, traditions, and religious beliefs of the people who lived there, a concept of community that approximated prevailing European ideas about civitas, and one that also distinguished communicentric views of the colonial era. To illustrate this point I will begin with a series of city views by the seventeenth-century Andean author, Felipe Guamán Poma de Ayala, before moving on to a series of other urban images, particularly those produced in the famous mining town of Potosí as they seem to exemplify views that mapped communities in ways that had little to do with the description of urbs.

.   .   .

Born in c.1546, Guamán Poma was a Christianized Indian from Guamanga, the modern Ayacucho, a town located in the Andean highlands of what is now Peru. After a brush with the law over certain land claims, Guamán Poma embarked c. 1600 on what he called his "world tour" settling eventually in Lima where, starting c. 1613 he began to write his massive *Nueva Coronica y Buen Gobierno de las Indias,* a treatise meant to enlighten the Spanish monarch about his Peruvian realms. Much has been written about the *Nueva Coronica* both as a source for native lore and as a pro-tracted exposé of Spanish mistreatment of Peru's indigenous popu-lation, but its chapter devoted to Peru's "cities and towns" has, with few exceptions, been ignored.[16]

In European terms, Guamán Poma's description of these cities combined a geography with chorography. Geography took the form of a *mappamundi de las indias,* "a world map of the Indies" that centered on the four provinces (or *suyos*) of the former Inca empire otherwise known as Tihuantinsuyo.[17] Guamán Poma's "world" was the Inca world, although the map he prepared to describe it was European to the extent that it employed a rudimentary grati-cule to pinpoint the location of individual towns: Santa Fe de Bogotá in the north, Santiago de Chile and Tucumán in the south. Guamán Poma, however, accorded special prominence to Cuzco, the for-mer Inca capital. In a symbolic demonstration of the city's impor-tance, he placed it at the center of his map between the escutch-eons of Castile and the Papacy.[18]

The chorographical section that followed was modeled after such geographical treatises as the *Civitates orbis terrarum,* as it incorporated brief written descriptions together with a series of city views drawn in pen and ink. Architectural historians have generally ignored these images because they offer little in the way of topographical specificity and detail, but they are of immense symbolic importance and provide crucial information about the idea—if not the "look"—of Peru's cities in the early seventeenth century.[19]

Whatever sympathy Guamán Poma felt for the sufferings of those he regularly referred to as the "poor Indians" of Peru, his urban vision was arguably more Spanish than Inca owing to the prominence it accorded to the central plaza or square, one of the defining features of Spanish urban planning in the New World. This particular urban model made its initial appearance in his sketch of the Heavenly City (*la ciudad del cielo*), a city whose squared design followed the Heavenly Jerusalem described in the Book of the Apocalypse and Augustine's City of God, although in this instance the multi-tiered fountain that stood at the center of the central plaza was based upon the one constructed in Lima at the start of the seventeenth century. The square is also lined with two churches and several other buildings, and these in turn were surrounded by a stout, crenellated wall inscribed with the words, in Quechua: "the city of God is for the poor who keep His commandments." The Heavenly City also enjoyed the watchful protection of God, his Son, and the Virgin. It appeared, in short, as a peaceful, orderly city, devoid of all manifestations of sin (Fig. 3).

In keeping with Augustine's ideas, none of Peru's earthly cities could compare with the *ciudad del cielo*, although each of these communities, with the notable exception of Cuzco, appeared in the *Nueva Coronica* as clones of the Heavenly City, that is, as a cluster of buildings huddled around a large central square. This uniformity is important because it suggests that Guamán Poma's conception of a city had less to do with urbs than with the character of its civitas, especially as it was manifested in the piety of the local citizenry, *policía*, and the particular manner in which local officials treated the native population. In other words, when he prepared his views of Peru's towns, he did so communicentrically, representing them less in terms of the peculiar characteristics of their urbs than in terms of the quality of their civitas.

On this score, none of Guamán Poma's cities were exactly alike. Some in fact were far superior to others, and Guamán Poma indicated these differences by introducing visual clues into the city views, using the plaza as the symbol through which the character of individual communities could be assessed. Some were patently evil, as in his view of Trujillo, in which two men are dueling in the central square. Others, like Chuquiapu, the modern La Paz, were cities of "policía, Christianity, charity, and neighborly love." Lima, meanwhile, the viceregal capital, was a city where "good justice" (*buena justicia*) prevailed, a quality that helps to explain why in his view of this city Guamán Poma used the potent symbol of the gallows to drive this point home. I should add that this view, except for the fountain, was totally imaginary: a dense cluster of large, multi-storied buildings that hinted at the city's importance. Particularly impressive was the outsized church occupying much of the view's foreground. Lima's cathedral, even in the seventeenth century, was large by Peruvian standards, but it was nothing like the building represented here which seems instead to represent what Guamán Poma defined as Lima's *cristiandad*. The corpse hanging from the gallows set into the middle of the square was yet another potent symbol as it corroborated his contention that Lima was a city where "good justice" (*buena justicia*) prevailed (Fig. 4).

Communicentric views of different sorts appeared throughout Spanish America. In some cases, they took the form of portrait views, an art form that combined two different artistic genres into one in an effort to express an individual's attachment to the particular community on display. Such views generally featured prominent creoles—of particular interest is the one of Doña Mariana Belsunse y Salasar now in the Brooklyn Museum (Fig. 5). Mariana, a prominent criolla in mid-eighteenth-century Lima, was a woman best known for her tumultuous personal life but one who is depicted here in a picture expressly designed to emphasize her wealth, social importance, and civic consciousness as reflected in the series of archways, an *allée* of trees, and a fountain meant to evoke the park (now Plaza de Acho) both she and her husband donated to Lima *c.* 1755.[20] As a portrait-view, the picture makes a bold double statement as it attempts not only to affirm Mariana's social position within Lima society but also to commemorate her commitment to Lima itself. Indeed, by drawing attention to her personal contribution to the embellishment of the city's urbs and pointedly ignoring all references to her private life, the painting seemingly endeavored to preserve her position within the civitas constituted by Lima's creole elite.

Somewhat more unusual are portrait views featuring native *curacas*, the native lords who in Inca times exercised political and religious authority in the rural communities scattered throughout

Peru. Although the Spanish conquest did much to undermine the *curaca*'s traditional authority, some, despite progressive Christianization, managed to reserve their traditional role of spiritual intermediary between their community and the world beyond, a position celebrated in a portrait-view of Chinchero, a market town near Cuzco (Fig. 6).[21] Here, the portrait-view forms part of a larger composition devoted to the coronation of the Virgin of Montserrat, a Marian incarnation that originated in Catalonia but one to which this community was particularly devoted. Completed in 1693, this painting, hung in the local parish church, was the work of Francisco Chihuantito, an indigenous artist native to Chinchero and one whose style reflected the exuberance of the *cuzqueño* school of painting. Evidence suggests that Chinchero's *curaca*, Pascual Amau, commissioned the painting to honor Chinchero's relationship with the Virgin and also to celebrate his own role as the community's spiritual intermediary with the divine. Measuring some four meters by three, the painting centers on the Virgin of Montserrat. She is seated, holding the infant Jesus in her lap, as two angels place a crown upon her head under the watchful gaze of God the father and the heavenly host. For our purposes, the most significant portion of the painting appears in the lower right, where Chihuantito inserted a view of Chinchero, represented, metonymically, by its church and adjoining atrium. This view also includes a religious procession emblematic of the local civitas led by the *curaca*, who is identified with the inscription "M[ayor]D[omo] Pascual Amau." Thus this painting, in addition to celebrating Chinchero and its particular devotion to the Virgin of Montserrat, commemorates Amau's position of leadership within the community together his traditional role of spiritual go-between for this world and the next.[22]

The religious procession evident in this painting brings to us another form of communicentric view: those in which a religious procession serves as a means of portraying civitas. Such images, commonplace in European art—Gentile Bellini's *Procession in the Piazza San Marco* (1496) is but one example—are rarely thought of as city views, yet, in a local context, they seemingly highlighted the way in which many communities wanted to see themselves, namely, as a *civitas christiana*, or holy community united by faith. Guamán Poma did just this in his view of Arequipa, which features a religious procession that was part of a local effort to halt the eruption of El Misti, a nearby volcano. Meanwhile, in Cuzco, local artists, in an effort to portray their racially heterogeneous community as a civitas christiana, displayed a particular preference for representations of that city's annual Corpus Christi procession, a festival that included representatives of the city's large indigenous population as well as members of the city's elite, both Spanish and creole. In one anonymous late seventeenth-century painting that highlights this procession, the city is mapped in two different ways: by its civitas, which was depicted gathered in procession in the city's main square and also by its urbs, represented, metonymically, by the cathedral (Fig. 7).

Much the same idea can be found in local representations of Potosí, the Andean town from whose mines Spain's Habsburg monarchs extracted much of their silver wealth. Founded in 1545 at the foot of what was popularly known as the Cerro Rico (literally, rich hill), Potosí, despite a harsh climate and the forbidding altitude of 13,200 feet, developed rapidly into a city whose population mushroomed to around 100,000 by 1600 and one whose wealth was transformed rather quickly into churches whose elaborate baroque facades belied the parvenu tastes of the miner owners who paid for them. In fact, Potosí was the South American equivalent of Carson City: a rough mining town rent by faction and feud and with little of the *policía* that Spanish towns in the Americas were supposedly to possess. Throughout the sixteenth and seventeenth centuries European artists and print makers tended to equate Potosí with the Cerro Rico, the source of its immense mineral wealth. On the other hand, they displayed little interest in Potosí as a town, which they generally portrayed in wholly conventional terms. In contrast, local artists, adopting a more communicentric perspective, reversed these polarities. For them, the Cerro Rico, Potosí's *raison d'être*, was important, but Potosí, as civitas, mattered more.

This is certainly true, for example, of Guamán Poma's view of the city (Fig. 8), which relegated the Cerro to the background of the view while highlighting a plaza surrounded by churches and several secular buildings. As such, the view bore little relationship with Potosí, a town whose plaza mayor—the Plaza de Regocijo— was by no means its defining urban feature. Yet by making the plaza, customary symbol of *policía*, the centerpiece of this drawing, Guamán Poma deliberately sought to present Potosí as a community that was utterly devoted, as he himself wrote, to "the service of God." The tranquillity of this plaza served also to corroborate the accompanying textual description where he unabashedly referred to Potosí's inhabitants as "good, honored and worthy people; Christians, they have charity, neighborliness, and they have many monasteries, churches and religious, and policía."[23]

The communicentrism evident in Guamán Poma's description of Potosí also appears in the work of other Andean artists associated with this mining town. Of particular interest is Melchior Pérez de Holguín (1665/70–1732), arguably the most accomplished artist in late seventeenth- and early eighteenth-century Peru and author of *The Entrance of Viceroy Morcillo into Potosí* (Museo de América, Madrid),[24] a picture that depicted the festivities organized by the municipal government in 1716 on the occasion of the viceregal visit (Fig. 9). In terms of its composition, the Holguín canvas represents what is perhaps the most complex communicentric view ever painted for a colonial Hispanic town, as it contains three separate scenes, each devoted to a different moment in the viceroy's reception and intended as a demonstration of what Potosí, as a loyal vassal, had done to receive this important royal official. The largest of the three features was the viceroy's ceremonial entrance into Potosí, and even though it included many interesting architectural details—the facades of the houses along the calle de Hoyos, the parish church of San Martín with its seventeenth-century facade and tower still intact—Holguín was less interested in Potosí as urbs than as civitas. The latter is represented symbolically by the clergy, members of the town council, and the noblemen, all of whom form part of the viceroy's elaborate entourage. Yet the civitas in this canvas also includes a host of ordinary onlookers, some of whom are pictured together with their servants, both Indian and black. Interestingly, Holguín inserted himself into this civitas, and in so doing made the claim that he, as a mestizo, belonged to the community his canvas depicted. Thus Holguín—a true local booster—sought to represent Potosí as a prosperous, racially heterogeneous yet harmonious community, a true civil society in the best sense of the term. The Cerro Rico, symbol of its riches and the source of so many of the town's problems, is relegated to the background of the small painting inserted at the upper left which portrays the ceremonial welcome that Morcillo received in the plaza mayor.[25] Yet here, as in the main scene, Holguín is interested in urbs only to the extent that it served, quite literally in the case of the insert on the right, as a stage in which Potosí, as a human construct, might be displayed. The overarching idea, it seems, was to create an image of Potosí as a festive community whose loyalty to the monarchy superseded the factional divisions to which it was ordinarily subject. Such an image was idealized, but it tells us a great deal about the way in which Holguín, and by extension other members of this community, visualized the community in which they lived.

A somewhat different communicentric view of Potosí—and the Cerro Rico—is provided by an early eighteenth-century painting, still in Potosí and generally known as the *Virgin del Cerro de Potosí* (Fig. 10). The work of an anonymous artist, possibly one of native or mestizo origin, the painting invests both the Cerro Rico and Potosí with a spiritual significance lacking in most eighteenth-century views of Potosí, particularly those by European artists.

This painting has been interpreted as one that encodes religious symbols of the pre-Hispanic era and supposedly refers to the cult of the Pachamama, Inca guardian of the powers of fertility of the earth and a goddess whose cult was widely diffused throughout the Andes, including the region around Potosí.[26] These Incaic elements may be present, but the painting is best interpreted as a historical allegory illustrating the discovery of the Cerro Rico in 1545 by a Christianized Indian named Gualpa and the foundation of the Villa Rica e Imperial de Potosí the following year. Variants of the story had existed since the sixteenth century and were recorded by a local chronicler, Bartolomé de Arzáns de Orsúa y Vela, just about the time this painting was done.[27] Arzáns repeated Potosí's early history in detail: how Gualpa, a shepherd, chased a runaway llama up the side of the mountain; how he lit a fire to keep warm; how he hunted a deer; how he pulled a bush out of the ground, revealing a rich vein of silver; and how a certain local *curaca* or native chief, Chaqui Catari, challenged his decision to reveal his discovery to the Spaniards.

All of the elements of this history can be found in this composition, together with the idea, also in Arzáns, that the Lord had refused to reveal the riches of the Cerro Rico to the Incas but had pointedly reserved them for Spain and the service of Christ. The artist, however, added another dimension to the story by transforming the Cerro Rico into the Virgin Mary, a linkage which centered on the notion of virginity and the idea that, just as the Lord was responsible for having kept Mary's purity intact, so too had he preserved the virginity of the Cerro Rico until the Spaniards arrived in Peru.

Virginity, and its attendant virtues, thus becomes the picture's dominant theme, and the artist drives this point home by depicting the Mary-cum-mountain at the moment she receives a divine blessing to bestow her inner treasure to the individuals assembled at her feet. These include, at the left, Pope Paul III, together with a cardinal and a bishop, neither of whom have been identified. The Emperor Charles V kneels at the right, accompanied by a knight of Santiago—probably Juan de Villaröel, the Spaniard to whom Arzáns attributed the foundation of Potosí—and a (Indian?) page, possibly Gualpa himself.

The final chapter of the story concerns the foundation of Potosí, a community whose urbs is portrayed somewhat hazily at the base of the mountain. That the artist inserted this view of the city within an orb is linked with Arzáns's contention that Potosí was nothing less than a "miniature world, a microcosm, the honor and glory of America, a world—like Rome, unto itself [*non urbes sed orbis*].

Such conceits, as this presentation has suggested, were typical of communicentric views, but in this instance they allowed Arzáns and other *potosinos* to "see" their town at the moment of its miraculous creation. In this sense, the painting constituted a 'map of meaning' that constructed Potosí from a symbolic as opposed to a cartographic or chorographic perspective. In other words, in the hand of someone who was apparently a local mestizo artist, the Cerro Rico that visiting Europeans of the period saw as little more than a topographical fact, a "space," became, for the locals at least, a "place" redolent with memories and traditions integral to their own notion of community itself.

Yet the Cerro Rico is by no means unique. There are other places—churches, secular monuments, plazas, walls, even mountains and fields—that stand at the center of communicentric views relating to other cities and towns. Such views were commonplace in other parts of South America as well as in other parts of the world, many of which still await detailed study. The important point to remember is that the meaning accorded to certain places cannot and indeed should not be separated from the people who experience them on a daily basis. Put another way, a gulf separates what might be called the "tourist gaze"—the guide-book's view of a particular region or town—from the insider's gaze, that is, the one shared by the local community and in which the lived lives of its inhabitants tend to revolve around what the British writer Raymond Williams has described as "the lived lives of a place." The difference between these two gazes—and, more broadly, the chorographic as opposed to communicentric view—is difficult to define, although Williams captures it beautifully in his novel, *The Border Country* (1960) where (with reference to a valley in Wales) he writes: "the visitor sees beauty; the inhabitant a place where he works and has friends."[28] In many instances, a difference of a similar kind separates maps drawn by professional cartographers from those prepared by the inhabitants of a particular locale. In this respect, what the cartographer renders in terms of a gridded and measured "space" becomes, in the hands of a local resident, a "place" imbued with experiences and memories that most outsiders, historians included, generally miss.

Figure 1. El Greco, *View and Plan of Toledo*. Casa del Greco, Toledo

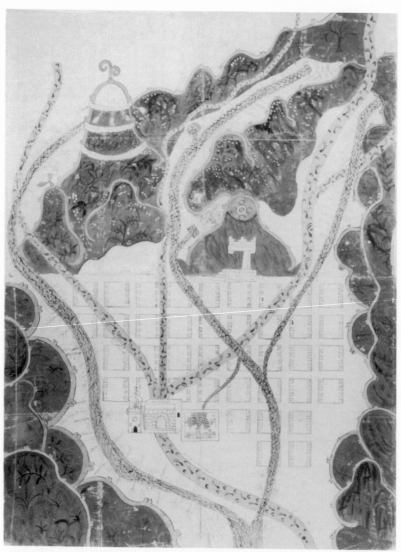

Figure 2.   Map of Texúpa. 1591. Real Academia de la Historia, Madrid

Figure 3.   Felipe Guamán Poma de Ayala, *The Heavenly City*

Figure 4.   Felipe Guamán Poma de Ayala, *Lima*, ca. 1614

Figure 5.   Anonymous, *Portrait of Doña Mariana Belsunse y Salasar.*
18th century, Peru. Brooklyn Museum of Art

Figure 6.   Francisco Chihuantito, *Virgin of Montserrat,* Parish Church of
Chinchero, Peru. Detail with view of church and town of Chinchero

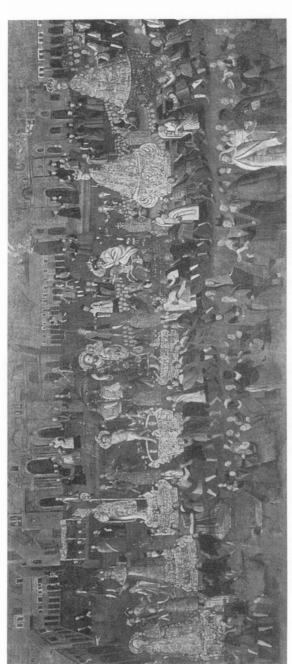

Figure 7. Anonymous, *Corpus Christi Procession in Cuzco*. 18th century. Museo Pedro de Osma, Lima

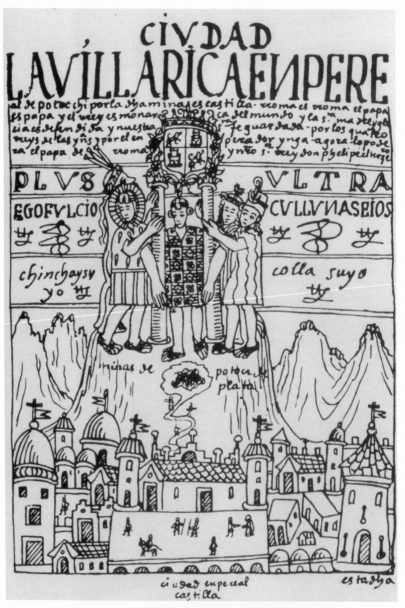

Figure 8.   Felipe Guamán Poma de Ayala, *Potosí*

Figure 9.   Melchior Pérez de Holguín, *Entrance of Viceroy Morcillo into Potosí*. Museo de América, Madrid

Figure 10.   Anonymous, *The Virgin of the Cerro Rico*. 18th century.
Museo Casa de la Moneda, Potosí, Bolivia

Notes

Portions of this essay have previously appeared in my *Urban Images of the Hispanic World, 1493–1793* (London and New Haven, Conn.: Yale University Press, 2000).

1. Juan Luis Vives, *De Tradendis Disciplinis* (1531) as translated in Foster Watson, *Vives On Education: A Translation of the* De Tradendis disciplinis *of Juan Luis Vives* (Cambridge, 1913), 41. See also Catherine Levesque, *Journey through Landscape in Seventeenth-Century Holland: The Haarlem Print Series and Dutch Identity* (University Park, Penn., 1994), 19. Levesque's approach to the seventeenth-century views of Haarlem, with its emphasis on an "insider's understanding of place," is analogous to my conception of a communicentric view.

2. Juan Luis Vives, *Arte de Hablar*, in *Obras completas*, ed. Lorenzo Riber (Madrid, 1948), 2:775, from Book III, chap. 1 "De la Descripción," of his *De ratione dicendi* (1532).

3. For more on these terms, see Richard L. Kagan, "*Urbs* and *Civitas* in Sixteenth- and Seventeenth-Century Spain," in *Envisioning the City: Six Studies in Urban Geography*, ed. David Buisseret (Chicago, 1998), 73–108, and Barbara Mundy, *The Mapping of New Spain* (Chicago, 1996).

4. For a brief introduction to these terms, and additional bibliography, see Richard L. Kagan, *Urban Images of the Hispanic World, 1493–1793* (London and New Haven, Conn., 2000), chapter 1.

5. Levesque, *Journey through Landscape*, 47.

6. Georg Braun and Franz Hogenberg, *Civitates orbis terrarum* (Cologne, 1572–1618), 3: Introduction. The translation is that of Levesque, *Journey through Landscape*, 46.

7. My multiple focus reading of this painting follows that of Victor I. Stoichita, *L'insturation du tableau* (Paris, 1993), 190–201.

8. For the Van den Wyngaerde view, see *Spanish Cities of the Golden Age*, ed. Richard L. Kagan (Berkeley: 1989), 130–36.

9. See Peter Jackson, *Maps of Meaning: An Introduction to Cultural Geography* (London, 1994). The sense of belonging—or place—I refer to here also approximates Aldo Rossi's "genius loci" (see his *The Architecture of the City* [Cambridge, Mass., 1982], 97), as well as Pierre Nora's "lieu de memoire," a site where local history and memory intertwine (see Pierre Nora, "Between Memory and History: Les Lieux de Mémoire," *Representations* 26 [Spring, 1989]: 7–25, and, more broadly, *Realms of Memory: Rethinking the French Past*, ed. Pierre Nora, trans. Arthur Goldhammer, 2 vols. [New York, 1996]).

10. For communicentric representations of Seville and other Spanish cities, see Kagan, "*Urbs* and *Civitas.*" For Mexico, see Mundy, *Mapping of New Spain.*

11. My understanding of the Greek and Latin origins of *policía* derives principally from Emile Benveniste's essay, "Deux modèles linguistiques de la cité," in his *Problèmes de linguistique générale* (Paris, 1974), 2:272–80.

12. In addition to Augustine, see Francesc Eiximenis, *Regiment de la cosa publica* (Valencia, 1499; fasc. ed., Valencia, 1991), whose ideas about cities are summarized in Antonio Antelo Iglesias, "La ciudad ideal según Fray F. Eiximenis y Rodrigo Sánchez de Arevalo," *La ciudad hispánica* (Madrid, 1985), 1:19–50. Aquinas's ideas about cities may be found in his treatise, *On Kingship. To the King of Cyprus*, ed. and trans. Gerald B. Phelan (Toronto, 1949), 68–80.

13. On this point see Gerónimo de Mendieta, *Historia eclesiástica indiana* (1595), ed. Francisco Solano y Pérez-Lila (Madrid, 1973), 2:87–88.

14. For communicentric views in sixteenth-century New Spain, see Mundy, *Mapping of New Spain*, and Duccio Sacchi, *Mappa del nuovo mondo: cartografie locali e de definizione de la Nuova Spagna (secoli XVI–XVII)* (Torino, 1977).

15. My interpretation of this map draws upon the text of the *relación geográfica* for Texúpa in René Acuña, ed., *Relaciones geográficas del siglo XVI* (Mexico, 1994), 3.217–22, as well as Joyce Waddel Bailey, "Map of Texúpa (Oaxaca), 1579: A Study of Form and Meaning," *Art Bulletin* 54 (1972): 452–72, and Mundy, *Mapping of New Spain,* 158–59.

16. Of several editions of the *Nueva Coronica* now available, I have used Felipe Guamán Poma de Ayala, *Nueva Coronica y Buen Gobierno*, ed. Franklin Pease, 2 vols. (Caracas, 1980).

17. Ibid., 2:354–55.

18. See Roleno Adorno, *Cronista y Príncipe. La obra de don Felipe Guamán Poma de Ayala* (Lima, 1989), 184.

19. Scholarship on these views includes Lorenzo Eladio López y Sebastián, "La iconografía imaginaria de las ciudades andinas en la 'Nueva Coronica y Buen Gobierno' de Felipe Guamán Poma de Ayala," in *América y la España del siglo XVI* (Madrid, 1983), 2:213–30 [a formalistic approach]; Jean-Philippe Husson, "Les villes peruviennes vues par Felipe Waman Puma de Ayala. Un Cas Particulier: Cuzco," in *La ville en amerique espagnole coloniale* (Paris, 1984); and Juan M. Ossio, "Guamán Poma: *Nueva crónica* y carta al rey. Un intento de aproximación a las categorías del pensamiento del mundo andino," in *Ideología mesiánica del mundo andino*, ed. Juan A. Ossio (Lima, 1973), 155–213. See also Raquel Chang-Rodríguez, "Un itinerario simbólico: Las ciudades y villas de Felipe Guamán Poma de Ayala," in *Libro homenaje a Aurelio Miro Quesada* (Lima: 1987), 1:320–36, and her more recent "Las ciudades de *Primer coronica* y los mapas de las *Relaciones geográficas de Indias:* Un posible

vinculo," *Revista de crítica literaria latinoamericana* 21(1995): 95–119. For purposes of comparison, see the maps and plans in Felipe Guamán Poma de Ayala, *Y no hay remedio*, ed. Elias Prado Tello and Alfredo Prado Tello (Lima, 1991), 42–44.

20. For details, see Ricardo Palma, *Tradiciones peruanas* (Lima, 1870–1915), 3.149–54, and *Converging Cultures: Art & Identity in Spanish America*, ed. Diana Fane (New York, 1996), 236–37, where it is reproduced in color.

21. Susan E. Ramirez, *The World Upside Down: Cross-Cultural Contact and Conflict in Sixteenth-Century Peru* (Stanford, Calif., 1996), 161.

22. This painting is briefly discussed in Pablo Macera, *La pintura mural andina, siglos XVI–XIX* (Lima: 1993), 63. For a somewhat more extensive discussion, see Kagan, *Urban Images,* 133–34, and Teófilo Benavente Velarde, *Pintores cuzqueños de la colonia* (Cuzco, 1995), 80–84. For other although somewhat later paintings representing *curacas* within the context of their village, see Teresa Gisbert, *Iconografía y mitos indígenas en el arte* (La Paz, 1980), 94–95. Of particular interest is the portrait-view painted on the panel of an organ formerly in the church of Jesús de Machaca, a village in a barren section of the Bolivian *Altiplano* some sixty kilometers southwest of La Paz. Dating probably from the early eighteenth century and executed in a naïve style that suggests indigenous influence, it depicts a *curaca* and his spouse kneeling, in a classic orants position, in front of a village, ostensibly Jesús de Machaca itself. The village is represented—metonymically in this case—by a stout church whose style resembles that of the parish church still in Jesús de Machaca today. Also included is a sketch of the church's large, open atrium and a few surrounding buildings. The *curaca*'s identity is not known, but by having himself portrayed praying on behalf of the community of which he was nominally head, he clearly sought to emphasize his traditional role as the village's intermediary between this world and the next.

23. Ibid., 2:404. The original reads: "buena gente honrada de valor, cristianos, tienen caridad, amor de prójimo, y tiene muchos monasterios, iglesias y policía, plata como piedra, oro como polvo, sin cuentos y sin millares . . . todo servicio de dios."

24. For details, see Teresa Gisbert and José de Mesa, *Holguín y la pintura virreinal en Bolivia* (La Paz, 1977), 185–96.

25. Compare this view of the plaza with the mid-eighteenth-century view by Francisco Javier de Mendizabal reproduced in J.T. Revelló, *Adición a la Relación Descriptiva de Mapas, Planos y Dibujos del Virreinato de Buenos Aires existentes en el Archivo General de las Indias* (Madrid, 1927), *lamina* lxv.

26. For this interpretation, see Gisbert, *Iconografía y mitos,* 17–21.

27. Bartolomé de Arzáns de Orsúa y Vela, *Historia de la villa imperial de Potosí*, ed. Lewis Hanke and Gunnar Mendoza, 3 vols. (Providence, R.I., 1965).

28. Raymond Williams, *The Border Country* (Worcester and London, 1960), 75, at the moment when Matthew Price, a Welshman living in London returns to Glynmawr, the valley in which he had spent much of his early life.

Index

Pages consisting only of illustrations have not been included in the index.